Winning Strategies for the World's Greatest Dice Game

OLAF VANCURA

tPuzzlewright Press and the distinctive Puzzlewright Press Logo
are registered trademarks of Sterling Publishing Co., Inc.

Library of Congress Cataloging-in-Publication Data Available

2 4 6 8 10 9 7 5 3 1

Published in 2010 by Sterling Publishing Co., Inc.
387 Park Avenue South, New York, NY 10016

Originally published in 2001 by Huntington Press, Las Vegas, Nevada
Distributed in Canada by Sterling Publishing
c/o Canadian Manda Group, 165 Dufferin Street
Toronto, Ontario, Canada M6K 3H6
Distributed in the United Kingdom by GMC Distribution Services
Castle Place, 166 High Street, Lewes, East Sussex, England BN7 1XU
Distributed in Australia by Capricorn Link (Australia) Pty. Ltd.
P.O. Box 704, Windsor, NSW 2756, Australia

Sterling ISBN 978-1-4027-7200-9

For information about custom editions, special sales, premium and
corporate purchases, please contact Sterling Special Sales
Department at 800-805-5489 or specialsales@sterlingpublishing.com.

Contents

Acknowledgments

I would first like to thank my dad. Our family has always played lots of games. In addition, he instilled in me a love of mathematics and taught me how to program. Little did I know that this combination would someday turn into a project such as this.

Thanks to Ken Perrie for originally suggesting the idea of adapting YAHTZEE to the casino environment and for many subsequent discussions on this topic. The requisite mathematical regulations associated with gaming prompted me to start thinking about the mathematical analysis of YAHTZEE.

Thanks to Dave Thompson, former CEO of Mikohn Gaming, who afforded me the opportunity to create exciting and novel gaming content, and Terry Oliver, my chief collaborator on many projects. In the gaming context, I first solved limited subsets of YAHTZEE.

Thanks also to a superb team of Hasbro executives, particularly Sonny Gordon, Lloyd Mintz, Pat Schmidt, and John Gildea. It has been a true pleasure working with such dedicated fun-loving people. They asked the essential question: Could the optimal strategy for YAHTZEE be ascertained?

Finally, thanks to Anthony Curtis, friend and publisher. I have enjoyed our many discussions concerning the mathematical properties of blackjack, YAHTZEE, and other games. This book is much better after your careful consideration of the material within.

1
YAHTZEE: A Brief History

YAHTZEE is one of the world's best known and most avidly played games. Now approaching its silver anniversary, it's estimated that more than 90% of all Americans are familiar with the name YAHTZEE and that it's played regularly by some 100 million people worldwide.

Although it's now a part of the American landscape, YAHTZEE is a game of humble beginnings. It was invented in 1954 by a wealthy Canadian couple while sailing aboard their yacht. They called their invention Yacht Game. Wishing merely to have copies to distribute to friends, the couple sold exclusive production rights to Edwin S. Lowe in exchange for the first 1,000 copies.

For reasons unknown, Lowe changed the name from Yacht Game to YAHTZEE, then began actively marketing his new product. One of his most successful marketing techniques was organizing YAHTZEE parties, which increased the game's popularity dramatically via word of mouth. Lowe profited handsomely, and in 1973, sold his company—and the rights to YAHTZEE—to Milton Bradley, now a subsidiary of Hasbro, Inc.

Over the years, the YAHTZEE family has grown to include several versions of the original game. These include Triple YAHTZEE (three games played at once), Painted YAHTZEE (die faces have different colors), Battle YAHTZEE (players duel), and Pyramid YAHTZEE (tetrahedral dice replace cubes). However, proving that some things may be better left unchanged, the original YAHTZEE game remains the public's overwhelming favorite.

Lowe Roller

YAHTZEE impresario Edwin S. Lowe's touch was decidedly less golden in Las Vegas. In 1962, Lowe bucked conventional wisdom by opening the first resort on the Las Vegas Strip without a casino. The $12 million 450-room Tallyho closed in 1963 and was replaced by the Aladdin.

2
YAHTZEE: The Rules

Before going further, let's get a handle on the rules of YAHTZEE. If you're already familiar with how the game is played, feel free to skip ahead to Chapter 3.

YAHTZEE's popularity is due, in large part, to its simplicity. The object of YAHTZEE is to achieve the highest score by constructing up to 13 different poker hands from the rolling of five dice. As the hands are made, they're recorded on the YAHTZEE scorecard. Each combination earns a specified number of points, which is indicated on the scorecard.

That's it. YAHTZEE is made up of two parts: playing the hands and recording the results.

The YAHTZEE Hand

The play of a YAHTZEE hand consists of an initial roll of all five dice and up to two rerolls. During the course of a hand, the player has a great deal of flexibility, as indicated by the following two rules

1. Any or all dice may be held or discarded prior to each reroll.

It's often desirable to change strategy in the middle of a hand. Consider the example on the next page. Your first roll is 2-6-3-3-2 and you hold the 3-3 (shown in black). With the 3s put aside, the reroll of three dice produces a 2-4-5, creating the hand 3-3-2-4-5. You may now change directions and hold the Small Straight of 3-2-4-5 (thus discarding one of the previously held 3s) prior to the final roll.

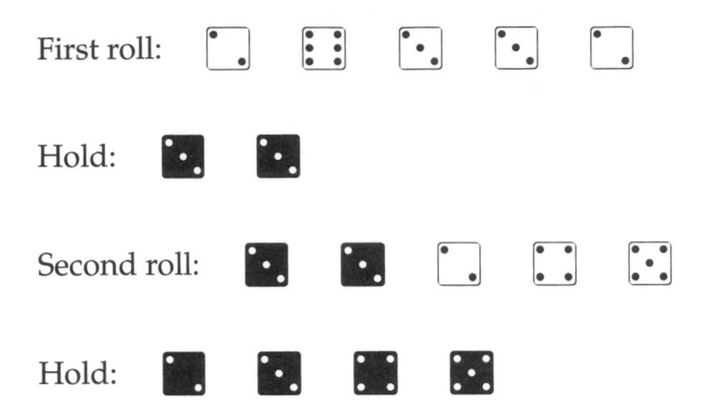

2. It is not mandatory to use all three rolls.

There will be times when, after either the first or second roll, it will be best to hold all five dice and end the hand early.

First roll:

In this example, the first roll has produced a Large Straight; you may hold all five dice and finish the hand without taking a reroll.

Review of the Scorecard

Let's take a closer look at each section of the YAHTZEE scorecard.

Scorecard—Upper Section

The top of the scorecard consists of six categories: Aces, Twos, Threes, Fours, Fives, and Sixes. Scores in these categories are calculated by adding all of the dice *that display the chosen number* in a finished hand. For example, the hand on page 10 can be scored as 6 (equal to 2 + 2 + 2) in the Twos box on the scorecard.

THE YAHTZEE SCORECARD

UPPER SECTION	HOW TO SCORE	
Aces = 1	Count and Add Only Aces	
Twos = 2	Count and Add Only Twos	
Threes = 3	Count and Add Only Threes	
Fours = 4	Count and Add Only Fours	
Fives = 5	Count and Add Only Fives	
Sixes = 6	Count and Add Only Sixes	
TOTAL SCORE	→	
BONUS	If total score is 63 or over SCORE 35	
TOTAL	Of Upper Section →	
LOWER SECTION		
3-of-a-kind	Add Total of All Dice	
4-of-a-kind	Add Total of All Dice	
Full House	SCORE 25	
Sm. Straight	Sequence of 4 SCORE 30	
Lg. Straight	Sequence of 5 SCORE 40	
YAHTZEE	5-of-a-kind SCORE 50	
Chance	Score Total of All 5 Dice	
YAHTZEE BONUS	✔ FOR EACH BONUS	
	SCORE 100 PER ✔	
TOTAL	Of Lower Section →	
TOTAL	Of Upper Section →	
GRAND TOTAL	→	

The YAHTZEE scorecard resembles the figure above. The results of each completed hand are entered on the scorecard. A score must be recorded after every hand.

Alternatively, this hand could be scored as a total of 4 in the Fours box or 5 in the Fives box. If necessary, the hand could also be used to record a total of 0 in the Aces, Threes, or Sixes boxes.

Notice the Upper Section "bonus." This is a very important part of the game, since a bonus of 35 points is awarded when the total in the upper portion is at least 63. The value 63 represents an average of a three-die tally for each entry. That is, 3 Aces + 3 Twos + 3 Threes + 3 Fours + 3 Fives + 3 Sixes (3 + 6 + 9 + 12 + 15 + 18) equals 63 points. Thus, the Upper Section entries are linked by this bonus consideration; if you're below average on one of the entries, you must achieve better-than-average results on another in order to obtain the 35-point bonus.

Scorecard—Lower Section

The bottom of the scorecard consists of seven categories: 3-of-a-kind, 4-of-a-kind, Full House, Small Straight, Large Straight, YAHTZEE, and Chance. The scoring for each of these categories varies, so let's take a look at them individually.

3-of-a-kind: A 3-of-a-kind is a hand in which at least three dice show the same number. The score for this hand is the total of all five dice.

For example, this hand may be used as a 3-of-a-kind with a score of 23.

4-of-a-kind: A 4-of-a-kind is a hand in which at least four or more dice show the same number. Just as with 3-of-a-kind, the score for this hand is the total of all five dice.

This hand may be used as a 4-of-a-kind with a score of 19.

Full House: A Full House is a hand containing three dice showing one number and two dice showing another (3-of-a-kind and a pair). The score for this hand is fixed at 25 points.

This is a Full House with a score of 25.

Small Straight: A Small Straight is a hand containing four dice in sequence. The score for this hand is fixed at 30 points.

This is a Small Straight (because of the 3-4-5-6 sequence) with a score of 30.

Large Straight: A Large Straight is a hand containing five dice in sequence. The score for this hand is fixed at 40 points.

This is a Large Straight with a score of 40.

YAHTZEE: A YAHTZEE is a 5-of-a-kind. The score for this hand is fixed at 50 points.

This is a YAHTZEE with a score of 50. Additional YAHTZEEs made in the same game must be used to fill another scorebox, but also earn a 100-point bonus (see "The Unique Nature of a YAHTZEE Hand" on the next page).

Chance: This is a catchall entry. The score for this hand is the total of all five dice. Any hand may be used as Chance.

This hand, if used as Chance, is scored as 20.

Scorecard-Filling Rules

At the end of each hand, one scorebox must be filled. And once a box is filled, it can no longer be used. In order to get the highest final score, it's preferable to fill in each box with as high a value as possible. But on occasion, one or more scoreboxes will have to be filled with a 0.

For example, consider a position near the end of the game in which only two scoreboxes are open: Aces and Full House. With the final hand outcome displayed below, we have a dilemma.

A score must be entered into either the Aces or Full House category, since one scorebox must be filled after every hand. However, the combination does not equal a

Full House, nor are there any Aces (1s) present. In this case, it's necessary to fill in a 0. It's your choice which of the two open scoreboxes gets the goose egg, but you will have to enter a 0 into one of them.

The Unique Nature of a YAHTZEE Hand

The best hand in the game of YAHTZEE is, naturally, a YAHTZEE. Provided that the scorebox for YAHTZEE is still empty, your first YAHTZEE is scored in that box and earns 50 points. Subsequent YAHTZEEs made in the same game earn a 100-point bonus. They are tallied by placing a check mark in the appropriate spot in the YAHTZEE scorebox. (Note that while the YAHTZEE box has room for only three subsequent YAHTZEE check marks, you are allowed to score as many YAHTZEEs as you make during the course of a game.)

Subsequent YAHTZEEs must also be tallied in an open scorebox, and a fair amount of confusion arises in deciphering the rules governing this requirement. Since YAHTZEE always qualifies naturally as a 3-of-a-kind, 4-of-a-kind, Full House, or Chance in the Lower Section, and also as its Upper Section counterpart (that is, a YAHTZEE made up of 5s can be used in the Upper Section Fives box), subsequent YAHTZEEs may be tallied in any of these open boxes, earning, in addition to the 100-point bonus, the points specified by that box's scoring rules. YAHTZEE may also be scored in either of the remaining two Lower Section categories (Small and Large Straight) according to the game's "Joker Rules," provided that each of two conditions are met: 1) the YAHTZEE box is filled (with 50 or 0), and 2) the corresponding Upper Section box is filled. If only noncorresponding Upper Section boxes remain, you have no choice but to fill one of them with 0 (see page 16 for the practical application of these rules).

Different Rules

The rules of YAHTZEE sometimes have slight differences, which vary by game version or release, even though they come from the same manufacturer. The explanations in this book come from the rules specified in recent Hasbro games. Of course, players sometimes employ their own "house rules," such as allowing a YAHTZEE to be used as a Joker only if it was scored as 50, or never allowing a YAHTZEE to function as a Full House. Regardless of which variation you play, none of these subtle rules differences alters the strategy advice presented in *Advantage YAHTZEE*.

If you make a YAHTZEE, but have already filled the YAHTZEE box with 0, score the hand in an open box in the manner described above. In this case, you earn only the score associated with the category that you fill. You may not score the 50 points for a YAHTZEE or 100-point bonuses for subsequent YAHTZEEs.

Sample Hands

Notice in the sample hands that follow that several scoring choices are possible.

This hand is a Large Straight (40 points). It can also be scored as a Small Straight (30 points), Aces (1 point), Twos (2 points), Threes (3 points), Fours (4 points), Fives (5 points), or Chance (15 points). If all of these scoreboxes are filled, the hand may be entered as 0 in any open box.

This hand is a Full House (25 points). It can also be scored as a 3-of-a-kind (13 points), Twos (4 points), Threes (9 points), or Chance (13 points). If all of these scoreboxes are filled, the hand may be entered as 0 in any open box.

This hand is a 4-of-a-kind (26 points). It can also be scored as a 3-of-a-kind (26 points), Fives (20 points), Sixes (6 points), or Chance (26 points). If all of these scoreboxes are filled, the hand may be entered as 0 in any open box.

Recording Additional YAHTZEEs

Lucky you! You've just made your second (or third or fourth) YAHTZEE of the game. How do you score and log the hand above?

If the YAHTZEE scorebox is filled with 50, take your 100-point bonus. If the YAHTZEE scorebox is filled with 0, you get no bonus.

You must now fill a scorebox and record the appropriate score.

Though the rules appear complicated, the best move tends to be straightforward. If the Upper Section Threes scorebox is open, it will almost always be best to enter a score of 15 there. If not open, the Joker Rules will usually be in effect, so choose the open Lower Section scorebox that earns the most points between 3-of-a-kind, 4-of-a-kind, or Chance (15 points each), Full House (25), Small Straight (30), or Large Straight (40).

If the corresponding Upper Section box and all Lower Section boxes are filled, you are forced to place a 0 in a remaining (choose the lowest) Upper Section scorebox.

3

Contemplating YAHTZEE Strategies

Part of the beauty of YAHTZEE is that every game is different. Much like chess, you'll never play the same game twice.

We have to wade into a bit of math to explain why this is so. Don't worry, the numbers are here simply to paint a clearer picture; you don't have to memorize them to use the strategies presented later (and there won't be a test) If this sort of presentation isn't your cup of tea and you want to skip the whole thing, I urge you to at least peruse the final subsection of this chapter—"The Variety of YAHTZEE." It will give you a feel for the enormous underlying complexity of this game that seems so simple on its face.

The Roll of Five Dice

When you roll five dice, you'll see many different outcomes. Mathematicians call each of these outcomes a "combination." A combination is a grouping of elements in which order does not matter. If we wanted to, we could list all the possible combinations of five dice beginning with:

1-1-1-1-1
1-1-1-1-2
1-1-1-1-3
1-1-1-1-4
1-1-1-1-5
1-1-1-1-6
1-1-1-2-2
1-1-1-2-3

... and so forth. Skipping ahead, the last few combinations would be:

4-5-6-6-6
4-6-6-6-6
5-5-5-5-5
5-5-5-5-6
5-5-5-6-6
5-5-6-6-6
5-6-6-6-6
6-6-6-6-6

In total, there are 252 distinct combinations that may be rolled with five dice.

Before proceeding, it's important to understand that not all of these combinations are equally likely. For example, look at the last two: 5-6-6-6-6 and 6-6-6-6-6. In a random roll of five dice, which of these two combinations is more likely? The intuitive answer, that the YAHTZEE is less likely to come up (making the first combination the more likely), is correct. The easiest way to illustrate this is to imagine that each of the five dice has a distinct color. Let's choose red, yellow, blue, black, and white.

Consider first the hand of 6-6-6-6-6. There is only one possible way to make this combination: All five colors (of dice) must land on the number 6.

Red	6
Yellow	6
Blue	6
Black	6
White	6

On the other hand, 5-6-6-6-6 has five possible ways of occurring. One way is for the red die to be a 5 and the rest 6s. Another is for the yellow die to be the 5 and the rest 6s, and so forth.

Red	5	6	6	6	6
Yellow	6	5	6	6	6
Blue	6	6	5	6	6
Black	6	6	6	5	6
White	6	6	6	6	5

So, for a roll of five dice (remember, order does not matter), the hand of 5-6-6-6-6 is in fact five times more likely than the hand of 6-6-6-6-6. We can say that the hand of 5-6-6-6-6 has five times the weight (5×) of 6-6-6-6-6.

A weight can similarly be assigned to each of the 252 combinations. For example, a hand of 1-2-3-4-5 is 120× as likely as a hand of 6-6-6-6-6, and so forth.

The Play of a Hand

Okay, we've learned that on every first roll, there are 252 possible outcomes. We've also seen that each of these outcomes has a weight associated with its relative probability. Now let's consider the variety of choices you may encounter as you play through the two rerolls.

To illustrate, consider a first roll of 1-2-3-5-6 and count the number of different strategies that may be adopted for this hand. To do this, it's useful to categorize the strategies based on how many dice are held.

We begin by holding all five dice. There are no decisions in this case—there is only one possible strategy.

Next we consider holding four dice and find five possible ways to proceed (an "x" denotes a rerolled die): 1-2-3-5-x, 1-2-3-x-6, 1-2-x-5-6, 1-x-3-5-6, and x-2-3-5-6. Each possibility is created by the decision to reroll a different die.

If we hold three dice, there are 10 ways to proceed: 1-2-3-x-x, 1-2-x-5-x, 1-x-3-5-x, x-2-3-5-x, 1-2-x-x-6, 1-x-3-x-6, x-2-3-x-6, 1-x-x-5-6, x-2-x-5-6, and x-x-3-5-6.

In the same way (without listing all the examples), we can determine that holding two dice also yields 10 possibilities, holding one die yields five possibilities, and holding none has only one possibility.

Phew! That's everything. Thus, there are a total of 1 + 5 + 10 + 10 + 5 + 1, which equals 32 possible strategies that may be adopted for the combination of 1-2-3-5-6, based on how many and which dice we decide to hold.

By repeating this exercise for each of the other possible 252 starting rolls, we can determine how many different ways the very first roll in a YAHTZEE game can be played.

THE VARIETY OF YAHTZEE

Performing the calculation described above for each possible starting roll shows that after just the first roll, there are 4,368 different paths the game can take!

Extending the calculation to encompass the remainder of a YAHTZEE game (13 hands of up to three rolls each), including placement in the scorecard and considering all paths of rolls and strategies, we find that there are something like 10^{135} possible different games.

Unless you're a mathematician, you probably won't grasp the unfathomable size of 10^{135}, which is a 1 followed by 135 zeros: 1,000,000,000,000,000,000,000,000,000,000, 000,000,000,000,000,000,000,000,000,000,000,000,000, 000,000,000,000,000,000,000,000,000,000,000,000,000,000, 000,000,000,000,000,000,000.

This is such an enormous number that even the impressive rows of zeros above cannot come close to conveying its size. Let's try to place it in context.

- There are about 90,000 (9×10^4) characters, including spaces, in this book.
- The population of Earth is about 7 billion (7×10^9) people.
- Bill Gates is worth some $50 billion ($5 \times 10^{10}$).
- The distance from the sun to the Earth in inches is about 6 trillion (6×10^{12}).
- An Earth-sized ball of sand might contain 10 million trillion trillion (10^{31}) grains.
- Even multiplying all of the numbers in these five examples together does not begin to approach the value 10^{135}.

Indeed, a universe-sized ball of sand might contain only about 10^{100} grains. Thus, we would need perhaps a trillion trillion trillion universes made entirely of sand in order to have a grain of sand for each possible game. In the context of these numbers, you might begin to get a handle on the complexity of YAHTZEE. While it can't be strictly stated that YAHTZEE is never the same game twice, the possibilities afford such unimaginable variety that it's appropriate to consider the game in a universal context.

Here's just one more way to characterize it. Assume that you've just completed a game of YAHTZEE. A supercomputer with the ability to play a trillion games per second, playing nonstop, would have perhaps a 1 in 10^{100} chance of duplicating your game in the next billion years. Even if you programmed the computer to mimic your strategy exactly, there would still be only a minuscule chance of duplication. Such is the variety in game play for YAHTZEE.

YAHTZEE's brilliant combination of simplicity (rules) and variety (game play) is what makes it one of the world's most popular games. Though it takes only a few minutes to learn, for the rest of your life you'll never experience the same result twice. Given YAHTZEE's mind-boggling complexity, how on Earth can we possibly derive the optimal way to play it? Read on.

4

YAHTZEE's Secrets Unlocked: The Optimal Strategy

The object of this book is to help you improve your YAHTZEE scores. The way to do so is to play as close as possible to the optimal strategy.

In mathematical terms, "optimal strategy" is the method of play that maximizes the expected score for a game. In laymen's terms, it's simply the best way to play—a recipe, so to speak, that tells you the correct play for every possible position in the game. Every possible position? How could an optimal strategy be derived for this monster of a game? That was the question that led to this book.

In March 1998, I had the opportunity to visit Hasbro's world headquarters in Pawtucket, Rhode Island. Prior to the excursion, I'd performed some back-of-the-envelope calculations, similar to those presented in the preceding chapter, so I was aware of YAHTZEE's incredible complexity. At a meeting with several Hasbro executives, I made the prediction that YAHTZEE would probably not be solved in our lifetime. In retrospect, that prediction was somewhat premature.

Over the next few weeks following my Hasbro visit, I toyed with the YAHTZEE puzzle. Could it be solved? Of course, it could in principle. It's true that a room full of monkeys, typing randomly into eternity, would eventually reproduce Shakespeare's *Hamlet*. That's in principle. In practice, it will never happen.

It's also true that a computer, properly instructed, would eventually play a perfect game of YAHTZEE.

There are only two problems. The first is time. As we've seen, even the most sophisticated computers can't play fast enough to crunch the numbers in anything approaching a reasonable time period. The second problem is that even if a computer did play a perfect game, who would know? For unlike the case of *Hamlet*, in which the target outcome is known, with YAHTZEE we don't know in advance what we're shooting for.

It was a conundrum: In order to get the optimal strategy for YAHTZEE, each possible position in the gargantuan universe of possible paths the game could take would have to be considered. Yet the greatest counting tool ever devised, the computer, was rendered ineffective.

There was only one way around the dilemma. The number of necessary calculations had to be reduced to a more reasonable figure.

A month or so after the Hasbro meeting I was driving from Boston to Mashantucket, Connecticut. U.S. Highway 95 is the primary corridor along the New England coast and, by coincidence, it passes within two miles of Hasbro's headquarters. Remarkably, it was while driving this stretch of road that I first envisioned the approach that would ultimately lead to the solution for YAHTZEE.

The Breakthrough

One of the keys, as it turned out, was to consider the game backward. By analyzing the game in reverse—actually starting at the point where all the scoreboxes have been filled and working back in time toward the first roll—it's possible for perfect choices to be made when faced with any decision encountered during a YAHTZEE game.

This technique of working backward is sometimes called "dynamic programming." In the case of YAHTZEE, it saves an incredible number of computations. This is because many of the billions upon billions of possible game paths become redundant and hence, at certain points in the game, a single calculation can be used to consider many different game positions.

Just because the task can be accomplished, don't get the idea that the chore becomes trivial. Even after eliminating an unfathomable number of paths, there are still about one million intermediate positions to consider. This still requires intensive computation. On a typical personal computer, the problem takes about two to three days—nonstop—to solve. Put into human terms, it's the equivalent of some 500,000 man-years of work. That is, it would take every person living in, say, Wyoming a year working nonstop (no sleeping) to arrive at the solution (or about four years if working standard business hours). The technique used to solve this mother of all puzzles is described in detail in Appendix III (page 124).

As fate would have it, I had the opportunity to meet with the same Hasbro executives again in May 1998, only two months after my prediction. Imagine their surprise when I announced that my original assertion had been dead wrong. Not only could YAHTZEE be solved, I was

The Last Bug

The original solution announced to Hasbro pegged 254.5 points as the expected score for optimal strategy. It turns out that an undiscovered bug in the computer code caused it to calculate the slightly errant result. The bug was discovered in early 1999, and computer analysis now yields the proper value of 254.6 points.

the one who'd solved it! The answer? With optimal play, a player's expected score is precisely 254.6 points.

Properties of the Optimal Solution

It's important to understand that the optimal solution is exact. There are no approximations whatsoever. No matter where you are in the game or what the current state of your scorecard, the perfect play can always be determined. It is truly the precise recipe for playing each and every hand in every imaginable situation.

The value of 254.6 points is also important. Knowing that it comes about by playing optimally means that there is no possible way that your average score (in the long run) can ever exceed 254.6. If you have a friend who claims to have an average score of 300, either he hasn't played very many games (and has been quite lucky at that), or (gasp!) he's prone to exaggeration.

As you might imagine, the solution itself is very large. To save it on a computer (in a human-readable format) would require about 10^{10} bytes. This is the equivalent of some 7,000 floppy diskettes or 7,000,000 typewritten pages. If bound into an oversized book, the thickness would be about a quarter-mile!

Properties of the Optimal Strategy

To better understand how a perfect YAHTZEE player performs, a computer was encoded to play 100,000 games using the optimal strategy. The remainder of this chapter provides important information gleaned from this, and other, computer runs.

The chart on page 27 displays the average value that will be scored in each category if you play perfectly. Note the high values expected for the Small and Large Straights, each worth about 30 points per game on average. This has to do with their relatively high frequency of

Expected Score Per Individual Category

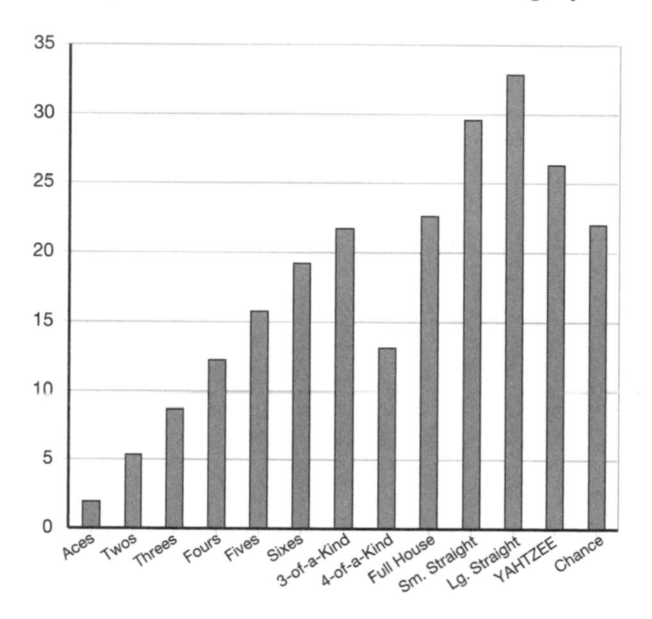

occurrence (especially for the Small Straight, which has only about a 2% chance of being filled as 0), and their high scoring values (30 and 40 points, respectively). The YAHTZEE category, despite being relatively rare, has a value of about 25 points per game, due to its high scoring value (50 points for the first YAHTZEE and an additional 100 points for every YAHTZEE thereafter).

Note too that the first six entries, Aces through Sixes, are arranged fairly linearly. Closer inspection reveals a slight bias toward Fives and Sixes (each with an average score in excess of 3× the number) compared to Aces and Twos (each with an average score of less than 3× the number).

The most glaring entry is the relatively low expected score associated with 4-of-a-kind. This is due primarily

Probability of Filling in a Scorebox With 0

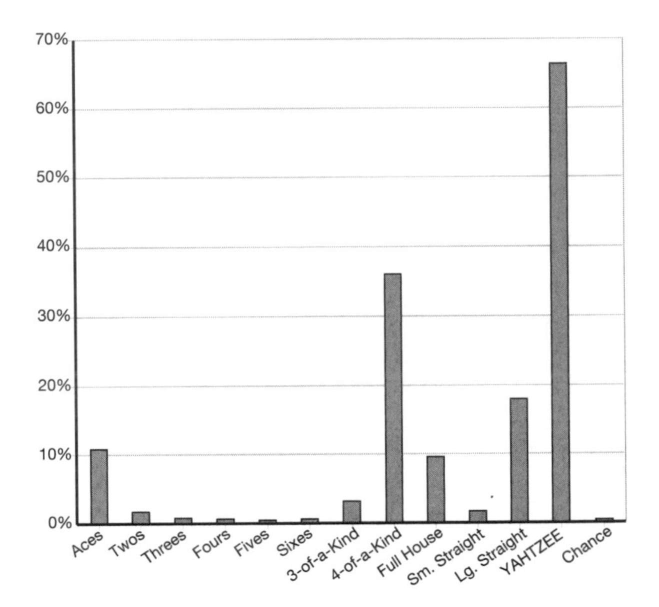

to its low frequency of occurrence (approximately one in three games will result in a 0 score for this entry).

If the dice always behaved the way you'd like them to, you would never have to fill in a scorebox with 0. But the fact that it occurs even for a computer playing perfectly proves that even with flawless strategy, it's sometimes unavoidable. It's inevitable that you'll play many games in which the dice simply don't cooperate.

In the chart above we see that the most likely category to wind up with a 0 is YAHTZEE. This is no surprise; YAHTZEE is the hardest hand to make. Also not surprising, especially to those with experience playing the game, is the high frequency that 0 is assigned to the 4-of-a-kind and Large Straight boxes. It's interesting to note that in

About how often does a perfect player:

• Score more than 400 points	1 in 35 games
• Score more than 300 points	1 in 7 games
• Make a YAHTZEE	1 in 3 games
• Achieve the 35-point Upper Section bonus	2 in 3 games

roughly 10% of games, the Aces box is filled with 0. This will be further discussed later.

The chart on page 30 shows the expected score for each open category as a function of how far along the game has progressed (hand #1 is the beginning of the game and hand #13 is the end). This is a key depiction, easily the most important chart of the three just presented in terms of the value of the information it contains. Just getting a general feel for how these values change will aid you in spots where an intuitive move is required.

Note that for hand #1, the values are identical to the values for the same hands in the chart on page 27. As the game progresses, several important trends can be seen. First, the expected value of all scoreboxes (except Chance, which can be filled in at any time, hence never has a 0 score) decreases with time. What this means is that the longer a particular box remains unfilled, the lower its average score is likely to be.

For example, consider the Large Straight. Whereas at the beginning of the game, we can expect it to score roughly 33 points, its value falls systematically as we play longer and longer without scoring one. On the 13th hand, with only the Large Straight left to fill, its expected score has dropped to nearly 10 points.

Expected Score Per Individual Open Category as a Function of Hand Number

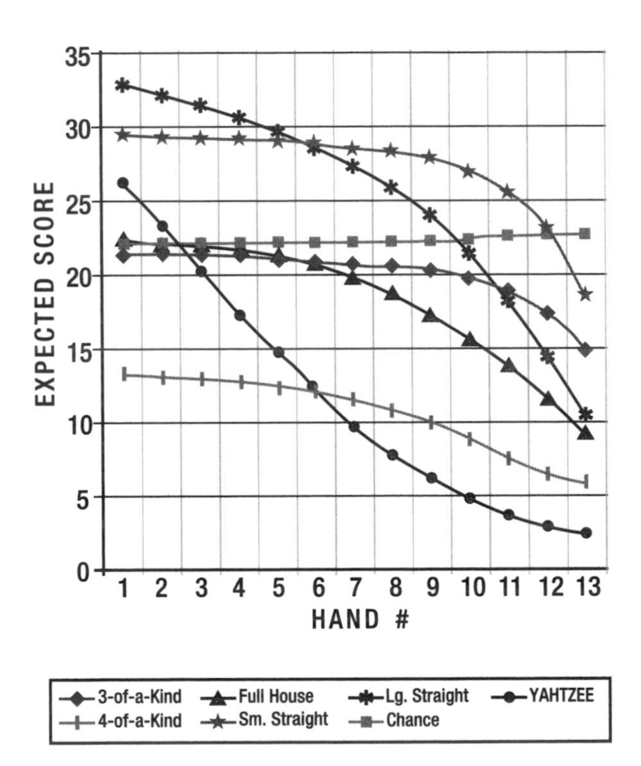

Secondly, the rate at which the expected scores of the entries fall is closely related to the difficulty in achieving them. Thus, the Large Straight and YAHTZEE entries, with their steep and consistent drop-offs, are somewhat difficult to hit at any point in the game. Conversely, 3-of-a-kind and Small Straight are relatively easy to catch throughout the game.

Finally, note that some of the lines cross each other. This illustrates how the relative value of an unfilled box can fluctuate as the game progresses. For example, if you had to fill in one entry with 0 early in the game, the chart tells you that the proper choice would be 4-of-a-kind (since early in the game it has the lowest expected score). However, given the same choice late in the game, it would be best to fill in YAHTZEE with 0 (since it now has the lowest expected score).

Later, when discussing proper end-game strategy, we'll come back to this chart to help us ascertain proper playing and scorecard-filling strategies.

Best of Games/Worst of Games

What are the highest and lowest possible scores for a game of YAHTZEE?

The highest possible score is 1,575. This would require making 13 straight YAHTZEEs (of the specific values needed to best complete the YAHTZEE card).

The lowest possible score is 5. You must purposely try to get this score by choosing to fill each category with 0. Eventually, you will have to fill Chance with the total on the five dice, whose lowest possible value is 5.

5
The Basic Strategy

While it's important to know that the solution to YAHTZEE has been derived, it's also important to realize that the precise solution, in and of itself, doesn't serve much practical purpose. It's too complex even to read, much less memorize. It's too vast even to reside in standard computer memory.

Up until now, we've been discussing the "optimal strategy"—the perfect strategy for maximizing your score. However, in order to realistically benefit from this complex strategy in actual play, we need to simplify it a bit. That is, pluck the important parts of the optimal strategy and present them in a more usable form. The resulting compressed strategy is called the "basic strategy."

The basic strategy is an approximation of the optimal strategy. Its purpose is to mimic the optimal strategy, while retaining sufficient simplicity so that it can be applied by mere mortals. Put another way, the basic strategy is a set of simple guidelines that grasps the essence of the optimal strategy, but characterizes it in a manner that can actually be put to practical use.

Chapters 6, 7, and 8 provide detailed treatments of the basic strategy for YAHTZEE. Learning and using it will almost guarantee an increase in your expected score. You'll notice improved results quickly. But before discussing the basic strategy in depth, we'll touch on a couple important preliminary considerations that can be applied to the whole game.

Types of Hands

With the exception of Chance, each and every scorecard category can be considered either an "X-of-a-kind" or a "straight." All of the upper categories can be considered X-of-a-kind hands, since the aim is to get as many of each value (for example, Aces) as possible. The 3-of-a-kind, 4-of-a-kind, and YAHTZEE entries are clearly X-of-a-kinds, while the Small and Large Straight are clearly straights. A Full House is a 3-of-a-kind plus a pair.

Though seemingly obvious, understanding that the game of YAHTZEE consists of only these two types of entries has important strategic ramifications. In particular, there are 10 different X-of-a-kind categories, but just two categories of straights. Given this reality, it seems logical that a winning strategy would embody a bias toward trying for the X-of-a-kind hands. And, as we shall see shortly, it does.

YAHTZEE Advantage Play

When given a choice, shade your decisions toward going for the X-of-a-kind hands, especially those in the Upper Section.

Sixes vs. Ones

Another fact is that higher-valued dice are worth more than those with lower values. For example, three 6s are more valuable than three 1s. There are several reasons for this. First, hands such as 3-of-a-kind, 4-of-a-kind, and Chance are scored by adding together all of the dice. So it's best to make X-of-a-kinds with dice of a high value. A 4-of-a-kind consisting of 1-2-2-2-2 is worth only 9 points, while a 4-of-a-kind consisting of 6-6-6-6-1 is worth 25 points.

Furthermore, in the Upper Section, you're trying to score at least 63 points in order to get the 35-point bonus. The added importance of higher-valued dice is obvious here. Getting ahead in the Sixes category (i.e., getting four 6s instead of the expected three) puts us six full points ahead of par, whereas getting an extra ace puts us only one point ahead. In addition, a deficiency in the Fives box is much more difficult to overcome than a deficiency in, say, the Twos box, and so forth.

Chance

The Chance entry is unique in that it's neither an X-of-a-kind nor a straight. It's simply the sum of all five dice. As such, it may be used at any time, with the knowledge that it will never have a 0 score.

When playing expertly, it is never proper (except near the very end of the game) to purposely try for Chance. Instead, this entry serves as a catchall in case things go awry. In other words, winning strategy dictates that Chance should be reserved as a safety mechanism only for an unwanted outcome.

Here's an important point. If given a choice between using a hand for Chance or for any other Lower Section category, it's always better to use it for the latter. For example, the hands of 4-of-a-kind and Chance are each scored in the same manner—namely, as the sum of all five dice. However, the 4-of-a-kind requires four dice to have the same value, whereas the Chance hand has no restrictions whatsoever. Thus, even with a "bad" 4-of-a-kind such as 2-2-2-2-5 (a total of only 13), it's never proper to fill in the Chance category if other suitable options (e.g., 3-of-a-kind or 4-of-a-kind) are still unfilled.

YAHTZEE Advantage Play

The expected value of Chance does not diminish during the game. Save it as long as possible for a situation that is unwanted.

6

Basic Opening Strategy: Hands 1 to 4

At the beginning of a YAHTZEE game, the scorecard is empty; all the scoreboxes are open and the possibilities are many. Given what you now know about the myriad directions a game can take, it stands to reason that your early choices will have great significance on your prospects for the entire game. How, then, should you approach the beginning of a game of YAHTZEE?

Opening Themes

The proper strategy at a game's outset can be summarized by three major themes:

- Follow the dice.
- Get ahead (or at least stay on par) in the Upper Section.
- Be opportunistic with "difficult" hands, such as YAHTZEE, Large Straight, and 4-of-a-kind.

Let's look at each of these three important themes in more detail.

Follow the Dice

One of the main themes early on is to take what the dice give you.

Remember, throughout the game you'll be trying to make hands that are either X-of-a-kinds or straights. Early in the game, it's not important to pick out specific categories and try to complete them. Rather, you should take the good scores that present themselves. The idea is to go with the flow. If a roll contains three or more of any particular value, it's generally best to hold those dice. Say the first roll of the game is 3-6-6-6-4. The best play here is the obvious one: Hold the three 6s. If the first roll is 1-3-4-5-6, then go with the Small Straight.

There's no reason to force the issue when the game is new. Just enjoy the luxury of being able to milk what you're given.

> **YAHTZEE Advantage Play**
>
> Early in the game, you should usually hold combinations containing three or more of the same value.

Get Ahead in the Upper Section

Early in the game, it's beneficial to get ahead as quickly as possible in the upper half of the scorecard. This improves your chances of netting the 35-point bonus for making a total of 63 points or more. Remember that 63 points represents an average of three numbers in each category (three Aces + three Twos + three Threes + three Fours + three Fives + three Sixes = 63). Thus, if you can get ahead by filling in one or more of the Upper Section categories with four of a particular number, you'll be well on your way to securing the bonus points at the conclusion of the game.

Final-hand combinations that contain 6s cause a lot of hand-wringing. A hand of 6-6-6-6-x should be scored in the Upper Section if possible. In fact, any 4-of-a-kind early in the game is best applied to fill a box in the Upper Section. Even four Fives or Sixes, which are very good entries in the Lower Section's 4-of-a-kind box, are better used in the corresponding Upper Section scoreboxes.

YAHTZEE Advantage Play

Use any early 4-of-a-kind in the Upper Section when possible.

What about 3-of-a-kinds? In particular, what about a final hand of 6-6-6-x-x? This hand, too, is usually best entered in the Upper Section instead of as a 3-of-a-kind. Remember that 3-of-a-kind is a fairly common hand, so you will likely have other opportunities in the game to fill this spot. Early in the game, 3-of-a-kinds are best applied to fill the Upper Section, which keeps you on pace to earn the 35-point bonus.

Be Opportunistic

Aside from YAHTZEE, the two toughest boxes to fill in the Lower Section are 4-of-a-kind and Large Straight. With respect to 4-of-a-kind, remember that the score for this hand is the total of all five dice. Thus, a hand of 1-1-1-1-4 (worth 8 as 4-of-a-kind) is far inferior to a hand of 6-6-6-6-4 (worth 28 as 4-of-a-kind). In the early stages, consider filling the 4-of-a-kind scorebox only after the corresponding Upper Section box is filled.

Remember that there are only two straight hands, Small and Large. The Small Straight is relatively easy to make and there are many opportunities to fill this box during the course of most games. Therefore, never keep three to a Small Straight early. For example, you wouldn't keep 3-4-6 hoping to get a 5.

Making the Large Straight is considerably more difficult. As such, when a hand with strong Large Straight potential arises, it generally makes sense to go for it. Given a hand such as 2-3-4-5-5, for example, the 2-3-4-5 is superior to the 5-5 alone. Notice that this possible straight is "open-ended," which means that it can be completed on each side (with a 1 or a 6). In a "closed-end" situation, e.g., 3-4-5-5-6, keeping the 5-5 is the superior play.

YAHTZEE Advantage Play

Never hold three to a straight early in the game.

The Toughies

Certain hands require a bit more flexibility in how you treat them. That is, they don't always adhere to the fundamental rules that have been set down thus far.

Two Pair

A decision that comes up frequently is how to play two pair. For example, it's early in the game and the roll is 2-6-2-6-5. Should you keep both pairs and try for the Full

House or keep just the higher pair and reroll three dice?

Since YAHTZEE has no category for two pair, keeping both means that you're going all out for the Full House—a Lower Section category. In keeping with one of the fundamental themes of getting ahead in the Upper Section, it's better to keep only the higher pair in this situation early in the game. If the scorebox for the higher pair is already filled, it's still better to keep the lower pair than to keep both. Keeping the single pair early allows much greater opportunity at the time that it's most beneficial to be opportunistic.

Small Straight + Pair—All Unfilled

When confronted with a roll that contains both a pair and a Small Straight (assuming Small Straight, Large Straight, and the Upper Section entry corresponding to the pair are unfilled), several factors have to be considered—among them, the type of Small Straight, how many rerolls remain, and the value of the pair. Based on the fact that a Small Straight will occur relatively frequently and a Large Straight will not, the rules below summarize the best strategy for this situation.

After the first roll: Keep the pair only if it's high (4s or better) and the Small Straight is 1 2 3 4 or 3 4 5 6. Otherwise keep the Small Straight. Also, keep all Small Straights of 2-3-4-5, regardless of the value of the pair.

After the second roll: Always keep all Small Straights.

Small Straight + Pair—Small Straight Filled

What if you encounter the Small Straight + pair and the Small Straight is already filled? Do you then keep the pair, or take an early shot at the Large Straight? Here's the rule.

If the Upper Section category corresponding to the pair is open: Keep the pair unless you have 2-3-4-5. This is true after either the first or the second roll.

If the Upper Section category corresponding to the pair is filled: Keep the highest single die after the first roll, and keep all straights after the second roll.

Full House

What if the first roll produces a natural Full House? This might surprise you, but on the first roll of a hand early in the game when the corresponding Upper Section and Full House boxes are unfilled, it's best to break the pat Full House and roll to the 3-of-a-kind. The reason is the powerful potential of this hand to make 4-of-a-kind or YAHTZEE on one of the two rerolls.

Faced with the same decision after the second roll, break the Full House again if the 3-of-a-kind is 4s or higher, even though there's only one roll left to improve the hand. Again, the intent is to improve to 4-of-a-kind (to get ahead in the Upper Section) or a YAHTZEE.

When a Full House is made after the final roll, always score it as such on the scorecard.

When you have a made Full House and the Upper Section category corresponding to the 3-of-a-kind is filled, still break it to roll to the 3-of-a-kind after the first roll, but hold the pat Full House after the second roll. In this situation when the Lower Section 4-of-a-kind is also filled, always keep the pat Full House.

Filling Strategy

At the same time that we're trying to get ahead in the Upper Section, we'll be filling in the Lower Section on an opportunistic as-come basis. If we stumble into a Large Straight or YAHTZEE, we'll always use it as such in the scorecard. Same for final rolls that result in a Small Straight or Full House.

Two Special Relationships

There's a special relationship between 3-of-a-kind and 4-of-a-kind, and between Small Straight and Large Straight. The primary reason for not filling in the 3-of-a-kind and Small Straight boxes too early is their frequency of occurrence. Since they're common hands, there's no great rush to complete them. However, there's a more subtle reason for keeping them open. Remember that their counterparts, 4-of-a-kind and Large Straight, are among the most difficult hands to obtain. By taking advantage of the relationship between these hands, you can increase your chances of completing the more difficult combinations.

Consider the straights. As long as the Small Straight is unfilled, you have great flexibility in going for the Large Straight. Usually, when trying for the Large Straight, you'll hold a Small Straight during the play of the hand. Now, if the Large Straight doesn't come in, the option to fill the Small Straight works as a good fall-back. However, once you've filled the Small Straight box, the quest for the Large Straight becomes more problematic. With the Small Straight filled, you're in a bind if you go for the Large Straight and fail.

The lesson to be learned is not to jump at the chance to fill in 3-of-a-kind or Small Straight. Flexibility is important. If you can keep these boxes open until their counterparts are filled, you'll maintain maximum flexibility.

SCORING THE TOUGH-LUCK HANDS

Alas, everyone will have bad luck sometime, ending with hands like 1-2-3-5-6 or 1-1-2-2-3. How should you enter dogs like these into the scorecard? This is a source of serious error among players. Never fear, *Advantage YAHTZEE* provides the answers.

Though it appears sparse, the list below covers every possible bad hand that you can encounter. Use it to assist you in scoring them in a manner that is least damaging.

Refer to the "Tough-Luck Hands" list when you get a hand that doesn't qualify for a Lower Section category (besides Chance) and contains less than 3-of-a-kind, making it undesirable for any of the Upper Section categories. Starting at the top, find the first condition that your hand fits and mark that score.

For example, given the hand 1-1-3-3-4, the best way to score it is as 2 points for Aces. The hand doesn't equal a Chance total of 22 (it's only 12), but it does contain two 1s, so this is the proper way to score it.

How about 2-2-4-6-6? The Chance total is only 20 and there are no 1s. Next on the list is two 2s, so it should be scored as 4 points in the Twos scorebox. A hand of 1-3-4-4-5 should be scored as a mere 1 point in the Aces category. The hands of 2-3-5-6-6, 1-4-4-6-6, or 2-3-4-4-6 should each be scored as Chance, and so forth.

It's instructive to know why a hand such as 1-1-2-2-3 is better scored as two Aces rather than two Twos.

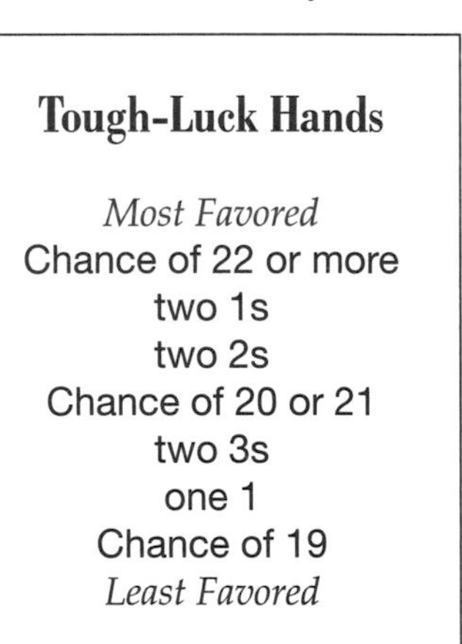

Tough-Luck Hands

Most Favored
Chance of 22 or more
two 1s
two 2s
Chance of 20 or 21
two 3s
one 1
Chance of 19
Least Favored

The reason is that later in the game, it's easier to make up a smaller deficit toward the Upper Section bonus. Recalling that you need to average 3× the number for each value, filling in the Aces entry with only 2 points (for two Aces) has a deficit of 1, while filling in the Twos entry with 4 points (for two Twos) has a deficit of 2.

An open Chance box provides a lot of valuable flexibility. You get a feeling for this when you consider that Chance should never be filled early unless the total is 19 or more.

Even filling in the Aces box with a value of 1 is preferable to exhausting Chance early. Late in the game, when you're trying to make your remaining open combinations, having the Chance option open will be a big asset. It's a common mistake for players to fill in Chance too early with a low total.

Finally, note in the chart that you'll never fill in the Upper Section categories of Fours, Fives, or Sixes with less than three of the number. Once again, the pursuit of 63 points and the Upper Section bonus is paramount.

Summary

- Be flexible. Early on, you want to go where the dice lead you, with a primary goal of getting ahead in the Upper Section.

- Be opportunistic. This is especially important with regard to taking early shots at getting the high-scoring tough hands. You will keep only two pat hands after the first roll early in the game: Large Straight and YAHTZEE.

- Preserve Chance. Try to save Chance for later in the game. It's the only category whose value actually rises as the game progresses.

Take a Quiz

Not all situations are specifically addressed in the basic strategy. However, a general understanding of basic concepts will often lead to the correct answer. See how you do on the questions below.

Questions

1. Is there ever a time when the first category filled should be Chance?

2. Is there ever a time when the first entry should be a 0?

3. When beginning a new game with a first roll of 1-2-3-5-6, what is the best hold?

Answers

The answer to question 1 is yes; a hand such as 4-4-5-5-6 should be used as Chance. The answer to question 2 is no; it is never proper to score a 0 on the first hand played. Another look at the "Tough-Luck Hands" list on page 44 will confirm these answers.

The answer to question 3 is to hold the 5 only! If you missed this one, don't despair: it's one of the least obvious decisions in the entire game, and very few players get it right. Early in the game, holding a high value is preferable to holding a lower value. The reason the 5 alone is better than just the 6 is that it enhances the potential for getting Straights.

7

Basic Middle-Game Strategy: Hands 5 to 9

The middle game in YAHTZEE is a time of fantastic complexity. At the beginning of the game, the scorecard is empty, so you know the situation you face, and at the end of the game, the scorecard is full. In between, though, the scorecard can be partially filled in myriad possible ways. Indeed, in the middle of a typical game—say, after seven hands have been played—there are more than 1,700 different ways in which the scorecard can be filled (considering only the categories themselves and not the scores they contain).

Due to the level of intricacy, it's simpler to discuss the middle part of a YAHTZEE game in general themes than it is to cite concrete examples. The variety in the game at this juncture makes the study of specific examples somewhat contrived, since it's incredibly unlikely that you'll ever encounter two middle games that are identical.

With this in mind, let's consider some of the strategic themes involved in playing the middle portion of a YAHTZEE game. Rather than be bound by rigid rules as in the opening game, you'll try to get a feel for how to best approach this most challenging part of YAHTZEE.

Overall Theme: Transition and Planning

We've learned that an important theme early in the game is to "go with the flow" of the dice. But whereas the dice dictate how you play and score your hands early in the game, in the middle it's necessary to start planning for the rest of the game. You still allow the dice to dictate your play—but only to a point. With several boxes already filled, you need to carefully assess the open categories as you play your hands, allowing a bias in the strategy toward filling the open spots.

The tack you take in the middle game depends, to a large degree, on your status in the Upper Section. Specifically, are you ahead, on par, or behind in achieving the goal of 63 points?

To ascertain your status in the Upper Section, add the values in the boxes that are already filled. Then calculate a sum for the values in the unfilled categories by assuming that you'll get three of each type. Add the two totals together to see where you stand. If you land at 63 points, you're on par. Similarly, if you have more than 63 points, you're ahead, and if you have less than 63 points, you're behind.

For example, say you have 48 points already scored in the Aces, Fours, Fives, and Sixes categories, and that the Twos and Threes are unfilled. Assuming you'll get three Twos (6) and three Threes (9), add 15 points to 48 for a total of 63 points (48 + 15 = 63)—you're on par.

When Ahead in the Upper Section

If you're ahead in the Upper Section, then you can afford to continue being aggressive in the middle game. For example, say you have the Fours, Fives, and Sixes filled, and are 6 points ahead toward the Upper Section bonus (i.e., the current Upper Section total equals 51 points). You can play more opportunistically to try to make the Lower Section combinations, knowing that even if you fail, you can afford to fill in less-than-perfect tallies for the remaining upper categories and still have an excellent chance of making 63 points and earning the 35-point bonus.

Assuming the conditions above, consider a roll of 1-1-2-2-6 with Full House unfilled. Early in the game you'd have kept the pair of Twos, in keeping with the rule of holding the higher pair. Now, however, it's better to keep the 1-1-2-2 because even if you don't succeed in making the Full House, you can fill in the Aces entry without falling behind in the quest for the Upper Section bonus.

In this same vein, you can sometimes try for a hand that you know will be difficult to make, such as 4-of-a-kind or Large Straight, knowing that you can record the score in the Aces or Twos categories as a fallback.

Though you're playing more aggressively, it's important to never fall behind the pace to secure the Upper Section bonus. Therefore, you must maintain vigilance while being opportunistic. For example, assuming you're ahead by 4 points, you can be more aggressive with the Aces and Twos unfilled than with the Fours and Fives unfilled.

When on Par in the Upper Section

When on a pace to just make the bonus, it's best to play similar to the opening game, with some strategic differences. First, it's necessary to consider what you've already filled. You'll have to proceed a little more cautiously so as not to put the upper bonus at risk. As the game proceeds, falling behind in the Upper Section becomes more and more problematic, as opportunities to make up the shortfall begin to diminish. As such, when on par, continuing to record an average of three of each value in the Upper Section is the paramount concern.

Remember that earlier in the game, with a Full House or a Small Straight + pair, preferential treatment was given to high values of dice. When in the middle game, and only on par for the upper bonus, preferential treatment should be given to any pair that corresponds to an unfilled upper category. As such, even lower pairs of Aces or Twos, if not already filled, should now be kept in the hopes of achieving three or more of that value.

As in the case of being ahead, if the opportunity presents itself to make a 4-of-a-kind (of Fives or Sixes when the corresponding upper category is already filled), it's generally correct to take the risk to do this. This is especially true if Chance is still unfilled, and hence can be used as a catchall.

YAHTZEE Advantage Play

In the middle of the game, if on par, take advantage of opportunities to maintain par in the Upper Section. Even pairs of Aces or Twos should be held if you need them and are otherwise on par.

When Behind in the Upper Section

If you're behind in the Upper Section, then the strategy is to try to make up the deficit.

Thanks to the opening strategy, you'll almost never be far behind in the Upper Section at this stage. Indeed, you'll usually be no more than 1 to 3 points in the hole. Remember, the opening strategy dictates that you don't fill in the Fours, Fives, or Sixes scoreboxes unless three or more of the value are present (see "Scoring the Tough-Luck Hands," page 44). Hence, you'll never be in a situation where you have a score of 12 in the Sixes box, because that means there were only two Sixes thrown, and the hand would have been recorded in another manner.

Note that sometimes—with bad luck—there will be situations in which, for example, the Aces and/or Twos categories have subpar scores. But these minimal deficits are easier to overcome. In these cases, you'll be trying to get a high 4-of-a-kind to use in the Upper Section to get back on par.

Still, overcoming an Upper Section deficit is usually not easy. There are times when the dice simply don't cooperate. However, even in these cases, our plan will be to stay close for as long as possible. Provided you can overcome the deficit with a single high-valued 4-of-a-kind, you will generally try to hang on to that chance.

Other Considerations

There are three other major cases to consider in the middle game. Each of these corresponds to having opportunistically achieved a difficult hand early in the game.

With Large Straight Filled
If you successfully roll a Large Straight early in the game, you can concentrate almost exclusively on obtaining X-of-a-kind hands. This is because the Small Straight is very common and can be picked up at leisure.

With 4-of-a-kind Filled
If you fill the 4-of-a-kind box early (as has been discussed, a 4-of-a-kind should be placed in the Upper Section early in the game, but there will be cases in which you roll another 4-of-a-kind of the same type), you can concentrate more on the Upper Section and on the Large Straight.

With YAHTZEE Filled

If you make a YAHTZEE early, you should play the remainder of the game slightly more aggressively in pursuit of the X-of-a-kind hands. This is because each subsequent YAHTZEE garners a 100-point bonus. As such, you'll generally hold 4-of-a-kinds (whether or not their corresponding upper entries are filled) in an effort to get another YAHTZEE. All 3-of-a-kinds will also receive preferential treatment—especially those that show up on the first roll. Pairs are unlikely to improve to a YAHTZEE and, as such, are not accorded special treatment.

SUMMARY

- Time to become less freewheeling. Begin giving preferential treatment to combinations that will help you fill open categories, especially pairs corresponding to unfilled Upper Section boxes.

- Accord special consideration to staying at least on par in the Upper Section. If behind, play for a high 4-of-a-kind (to score in the Upper Section) that will help you catch up.

- Press your advantage when you've made big hands early. If you made a Large Straight, try only for X-of-a-kind hands, since the Small Straight is easy to pick up. If you make a YAHTZEE, be more aggressive going for additional YAHTZEEs.

8

Basic End-Game Strategy: Hands 10 to 13

The YAHTZEE end game is more than just a mop-up job. In fact, the last few hands of the game are highly strategic.

First, you'll need to force the issue; with only a few scoreboxes left unfilled, you'll need to aggressively try to make these specific hands.

Second, because only a few scoring boxes are left open, you may on occasion end up with a hand that does not correspond to any of the available categories. As such, you'll be forced to fill in a 0 somewhere. Knowing the proper order in which you should fill categories with 0s is critical.

In identical situations, with one or two hands left to play, a skilled end-game player can wind up with 10 or more extra points than an unskilled player. The difference is knowing the proper strategy relative to your position. Let's take a look at expert play near the end of the game.

Forcing the Issue

You are generally playing the end game with the last few unfilled categories in mind. At this point, instead of "taking what the dice give you," as was appropriate in the opening game, it's necessary to force the issue. Desperate measures will sometimes become necessary. At this point, you'll have to scramble as necessary to optimize your last few rolls.

For example, if you have only Large Straight and 4-of-a-kind left to fill, and the first roll is 1-2-4-5-6, you should keep the 2-4-5-6 (or 1-2-4-5) and try for the Large Straight. Early in the game, you would never take this route. But with time running out at the end of the game, it's now or never to fill the remaining open scoreboxes. Needing only one more number to make the Large Straight forces you to try for it at this point.

As another example, if only the Fours and Aces boxes are unfilled, and (with no prior YAHTZEE) you roll 2-4-5-5-6, you should keep only the 4. This is a horrible play early, but in the end game, desperately in need of 4s, it's the proper play.

End-Game Considerations

We can learn a lot about proper end-game play by starting at the very end. With one unfilled scorebox, there's one hand left to be played and you're shooting for a particular outcome. For example, you may need a Large Straight or four (or more) 2s.

Strategically, the play of the hand becomes fairly apparent. For example, if the Fours box is the only one unfilled, your goal will be to roll 4s. If Chance is the only unfilled scorebox, your goal will be to roll high numbers. And so forth.

Let's begin with a simple question. Assume your scorecard is complete except for one box: Large Straight. That is, you have one hand left to play, and if you can make a Large Straight, you'll get 40 points. However, if you don't make the hand, you'll have to take 0 points for this last box, since the rest of your scorecard is already full. Of course, you won't always make the Large Straight. So, on average, how many points is this unfilled category really worth? Put another way, what is the expected value for the last hand, knowing that you need a Large Straight?

Through computer analysis, it can be determined that the expected value is 10.6 points, and dividing the 10.6 by 40 provides an estimate of how often the Large Straight will be made—about 27% of the time, assuming perfect play in trying to achieve it.

It may surprise you to learn that an unfilled Small Straight (although worth only 30 points) actually has a higher expected value. In instances where it's the Small Straight or nothing, you'll succeed about 62% of the time, which yields an expected value of 18.5 points. This means that an empty Small Straight box is worth more than an empty Large Straight box. Specifically, it's worth about 8 extra points to your total score.

So, if you are presented with a situation in which only the two boxes of Small and Large Straight are unfilled, and you must choose one of them to fill with 0, what should you do?

Consider the game-in-progress shown on the next page. Let's assume you've just finished playing the 12th hand and the final outcome was 3-3-4-4-5. This is neither a Small Straight nor a Large Straight, but one of those two boxes must be filled with 0. If you fill Small Straight with 0, then the expected value for the last hand is 10.6 points (since only Large Straight is left unfilled). However, if you fill Large Straight with 0, then the expected value for the last hand is 18.5 points (since only Small Straight is left unfilled). To maximize your expected score, the correct answer, is to fill Large Straight with 0, hoping to achieve a Small Straight on the final hand.

Putting 0 in a box with a potential of 40 points as opposed to one with 30 points may be difficult to do. However, it's not merely the potential value of an entry that's important, it's also the likelihood that you'll achieve it. That's why it's more valuable to preserve the Small Straight than the Large Straight late in the game. This

UPPER SECTION		HOW TO SCORE	
Aces	⚀ = 1	Count and Add Only Aces	3
Twos	⚁ = 2	Count and Add Only Twos	8
Threes	⚂ = 3	Count and Add Only Threes	6
Fours	⚃ = 4	Count and Add Only Fours	16
Fives	⚄ = 5	Count and Add Only Fives	15
Sixes	⚅ = 6	Count and Add Only Sixes	18
TOTAL SCORE		→	66
BONUS		If total score is 63 or over SCORE 35	35
TOTAL		Of Upper Section →	101

LOWER SECTION			
3-of-a-kind		Add Total of All Dice	22
4-of-a-kind		Add Total of All Dice	21
Full House		SCORE 25	25
Sm. Straight	Sequence of 4	SCORE 30	
Lg. Straight	Sequence of 5	SCORE 40	
YAHTZEE	5-of-a-kind	SCORE 50	0
Chance		Score Total of All 5 Dice	23
YAHTZEE BONUS		✔ FOR EACH BONUS	
		SCORE 100 PER ✔	
TOTAL	Of Lower Section	→	
TOTAL	Of Upper Section	→	101
GRAND TOTAL		→	

analysis can be used to make decisions involving any final two Lower Section categories.

The table on the next page lists the expected value of each Lower Section category when left as the last one unfilled with one hand remaining. (The Upper Section categories also have known final hand expected values. The

Expected Score Per Last Unfilled Scorecard Entry
Lower Section Categories

Category	Expected Score
Chance	23.3
Small Straight	18.5
3-of-a-kind	15.2
Large Straight	10.6
Full House	9.2
4-of-a-kind	5.6
YAHTZEE	2.3

last-hand comparison when both an Upper and Lower Section category are involved is discussed later in this chapter.) By comparing the values, you can determine the order in which the categories in the Lower Section should be filled with 0.

Late in the game, start at the bottom and score the 0 in the first open category that you encounter. The key order to remember is YAHTZEE, then 4-of-a-kind, Full House, and Large Straight. By referring to the chart on page 30, you can see that the same ordering is proper not just for the last hand, but for most of the end game.

In the example on page 56, a previous YAHTZEE has not been recorded (indicated by the YAHTZEE scorebox being filled with 0). Had there been a previous YAHTZEE, however, the absolute value of each hand would rise slightly (owing to the bonus if another YAHTZEE is achieved), but the relative ranking of the entries would not change appreciably.

Now let's look at the Upper Section scorecard entries. If your only goal on the next hand is to fill in Aces, how

Expected Score Per
Last Unfilled Scorecard Entry
Upper Section Categories

Aces	2.1
Twos	4.2
Threes	6.3
Fours	8.4
Fives	10.5
Sixes	12.6

many, on average, will you roll? It turns out that the answer is 2.1. In fact, 2.1 is the average for each of the Upper Section categories. So, for example, if only the Sixes box is unfilled, the expected score is 2.1 × 6 = 12.6 points.

When playing the end game, it's usually important to know where you stand in pursuit of the bonus in the Upper Section. For example, if the Upper Section scorecard stands at 60 points (3 points shy of the necessary 63), and the only category unfilled is Aces, you need three Aces. If this is your only goal, the chance you'll get three or more aces in one hand is about 35%. On the other hand, if the only unfilled box is Threes (hence you need just one 3 to get the bonus), there's about a 94% chance of success. The following table summarizes the probabilities of rolling a prescribed number of dice displaying the same (prespecified) value.

Note that it's a fairly safe bet to assume that you'll get at least two of a needed value, but not so safe for three or more if only one hand is left to be played.

Distribution for Rolling a Prescribed Number of Same Value

Total	Probability
At least one	93.51%
At least two	69.89%
At least three	35.49%
At least four	10.45%
Five	1.33%

Abandoning the Quest for the Upper Section Bonus

On occasion, the quest for the Upper Section bonus will have to be abandoned late in the game. The exact point at which this occurs is difficult to pinpoint. Every game is different, and the exact timing is a sensitive function of the hands remaining and the scoring boxes left unfilled.

Because in principle we don't want to unnecessarily harm our chances of getting an Upper Section bonus of 35 points, it's usually preferable—if we have to put a 0 somewhere on the scorecard—to put it in the Lower Section. However, there are two cases in which a 0 may properly be put in the Upper Section. The first is if you are comfortably ahead in (or have clinched) your quest to reach 63 points. The second is if you are way behind. In either case, it's correct to score Aces or Twos as 0 before 4-of-a-kind, Full House, or Large Straight. Similarly, Threes may be scored as 0 before Full House or Large Straight. In all other cases, including those in which there is still an outside chance of making the Upper Section bonus, if an entry must be filled with 0, putting it in the Lower Section is preferred.

With this in mind, if late in the game there are two Upper Section categories unfilled, and you need three of one type and four of the other to reach the bonus, your chance of succeeding is slim. In general, it's safe to say that with just a few hands remaining, if you're still behind in the Upper Section, then you probably won't be getting the 35-point bonus. As such, you're better off concentrating on completing the other portions of the scorecard to your best advantage.

One additional consideration comes into play when you are playing against opponents. When your primary goal is to win the game, it will at times be necessary to deviate slightly from this advice in order to optimize your likelihood of victory (see Chapter 9).

Finally, Those Blasted Zero Entries

It's not uncommon for one or more boxes to be filled with 0 at the end of the game. This is not a sign of poor play. Quite the contrary, it's to be expected. Even when playing optimally, it's very likely that one or more entries will be filled with 0.

This can be seen in the annotated "perfect" games that appear later in this book. Although those games are played using the optimal strategy (hence, perfectly), the appearance of 0 entries is commonplace.

Summary

- When necessary, fill scoreboxes with 0s according to each category's expected score. Don't hesitate to fill YAHTZEE with zero before the other categories; its value diminishes rapidly as the game winds down.

- Preserve your chance of making the Upper Section bonus for as long as possible, but be prepared to abandon it when the odds become prohibitive.

- Force the issue on the last few unfilled categories. Be willing to hold combinations that you wouldn't hold early in order to maximize your chances.

9

Playing Against Others

The optimal strategy discussed in this book is the recipe for maximizing your expected score. That is, if you could play the optimal strategy perfectly, you would obtain the highest possible average score per game. The basic strategy provided in these pages approximates the optimal strategy. Hence, playing according to the *Advantage YAHTZEE* recommendations will similarly optimize the goal of improving your average score.

When playing with others, however, your goal may be a little different. Specifically, your main objective will probably be to win the game. You may, in fact, have little regard for your actual score, as long as it's higher than the scores of your opponents.

Note that if you were to play a large number of games against your opponents, recording each score, then adding them all up to determine who was the winner, then the strategy presented in this book would be the one to adopt. However, the play of a single game is subject to fluctuations in outcome. For example, if you're lucky you may get a YAHTZEE early on. If you're unlucky, you may fail to get a Large Straight or the Upper Section bonus, despite nearly perfect play.

It's a fact that when playing one or more opponents and trying to achieve the highest score in the group, your strategy is likely to deviate somewhat from the optimal strategy. That is, your opponents' styles, and ultimately their results, will often force you to adopt a different strategy—one that maximizes your chances of achieving a new goal of, in most cases, catching up to your competitors.

Here's an example of switching strategies based on available information. For this example, we'll play a simple game (not YAHTZEE) with a single die. The object is to make the highest total. After one roll, you may either keep the first result or choose a single reroll. Your score is the value of the die you end up with. The average value for a roll is 3.5 (the average of the sum of the totals 1 through 6). So the optimal strategy after the first roll is to keep a 4 or higher and reroll a 3 or lower. Playing in this manner, the optimal strategy yields an expected score of 4.25.

However, assume you're up against an opponent. He goes first, rolls a 5, and keeps this score. Now the strategy described above is no longer optimal. That's because a first roll of 4 is not good enough once you know your opponent has 5. You need to play more aggressively, which means adopting a new strategy. Instead of keeping a 4 or higher after the first roll, you need to keep a 5 or higher.

On the other hand, if your opponent goes first, rolls a 3, and announces he'll reroll (after your turn is finished), then you don't need to modify the strategy. His average score after the second roll will be 3.5. If you simply stick to the optimal strategy, your expected score will be 4.25 and you'll wind up ahead.

In YAHTZEE, the situation is analogous: You should stay with the *Advantage YAHTZEE* basic strategy until your opponents' scores dictate otherwise. Since you have no information about your opponents' results at the start of the game, your play should closely mimic that set forth in Chapter 6. Monitor the game's progress to determine whether or not, and when, it becomes proper to deviate. If you're leading your opponents or within reasonable striking distance with time to play, there's usually no reason to depart from the strategies presented in this book. However, if one of your opponents takes a lead, especially a significant one (perhaps he rolls a YAHTZEE), then you will need to modify your strategy fairly quickly to enhance your chances of making up the difference. In this situation, you're unlikely to make up a 50-point disadvantage unless you also make a YAHTZEE, so you will have to try for it more aggressively.

You don't have to overcompensate dramatically if it's early. If you continue to play according to *Advantage YAHTZEE* precepts and secure the Upper Section bonus, it may become evident that your opponent will not achieve his bonus and you will have cut the deficit to 15 points (at which point the formulating of yet another strategy may be necessary).

However, as you get into the later stages of the game still behind, be prepared to do almost anything. You may reach a point where you need back-to-back YAHTZEEs to win. If this is your only chance (a 1-in-500 shot), go for it. Of course you won't even have this small hope if you've killed that one chance by filling the YAHTZEE scorebox with a 0 earlier on. If an opponent makes a YAHTZEE, it's important to preserve the YAHTZEE scorebox until you determine that you can win without it.

Playing to Win

As a general model for playing against competitors, proceed as follows:

1. Begin by playing the *Advantage YAHTZEE* basic strategy.
2. Monitor your opponents' progress.
3. If close to even or ahead of your opponents, stay with the basic strategy.
4. If behind your opponents, depart from the basic strategy and aggressively try to make up the difference.

Appendix I

How Did You Do?

By now you know that the expected score with optimal play is 254.6. Over time, you can achieve no higher average. However, many scores, higher and lower, will be tallied on the way to this average, and it's interesting to see where they land in the universe of all possible scores. The chart in this Appendix gives you the answer. By comparing your score with the corresponding percentage in the chart, you can determine how well, or poorly, you've just done.

For example, a score of 342 corresponds to 92.469%. Hence, your score is better than all but about 7.5% of the scores that can be made (assuming computer-perfect play). On the other side of the coin, a score of 205 puts you at 17.869%, which means that slightly better than four out of five players (assuming computer-perfect play) will score higher than you.

It's interesting to note that the score closest to the optimal average (255), falls at the 56.690% point in the distribution, which indicates that you are more likely to score under that mark than over it. On the other hand, your high scores will, on average, exceed 255 by slightly more than your low scores will fall short of 255.

Use the chart (and the curve on page 70) to gauge your results after playing a game of YAHTZEE.

Score	%ile	Score	%ile	Score	%ile	Score	%ile
<151	<1.000	190	8.124	231	33.981	272	75.581
		191	8.590	232	34.559	273	76.420
151	1.099	192	9.088	233	35.223	274	77.153
152	1.189	193	9.609	234	35.898	275	77.835
153	1.303	194	10.154	235	36.667	276	78.411
154	1.422	195	10.747	236	37.538	277	78.908
155	1.543	196	11.397	237	38.442	278	79.357
156	1.645	197	12.095	238	39.415	279	79.733
157	1.758	198	12.822	239	40.563	280	80.068
158	1.887	199	13.568	240	41.774	281	80.385
159	1.995	200	14.346	241	43.023	282	80.693
160	2.107	201	15.142	242	44.267	283	80.962
161	2.244	202	15.907	243	45.483	284	81.221
162	2.385	203	16.585	244	46.612	285	81.508
163	2.517	204	17.236	245	47.751	286	81.771
164	2.640	205	17.869	246	48.825	287	82.072
165	2.754	206	18.518	247	49.824	288	82.390
166	2.866	207	19.113	248	50.763	289	82.718
167	2.990	208	19.701	249	51.656	290	83.062
168	3.136	209	20.295	250	52.475	291	83.415
169	3.271	210	20.837	251	53.331	292	83.763
170	3.419	211	21.391	252	54.136	293	84.113
171	3.579	212	21.987	253	54.997	294	84.395
172	3.725	213	22.604	254	55.879	295	84.680
173	3.901	214	23.211	255	56.690	296	84.940
174	4.072	215	23.873	256	57.549	297	85.193
175	4.240	216	24.557	257	58.477	298	85.432
176	4.422	217	25.232	258	59.462	299	85.637
177	4.620	218	25.868	259	60.440	300	85.832
178	4.793	219	26.565	260	61.524	301	86.030
179	4.968	220	27.247	261	62.643	302	86.230
180	5.176	221	27.898	262	63.860	303	86.416
181	5.390	222	28.563	263	65.099	304	86.601
182	5.609	223	29.194	264	66.325	305	86.816
183	5.828	224	29.768	265	67.654	306	87.032
184	6.103	225	30.373	266	68.943	307	87.266
185	6.371	226	30.976	267	70.141	308	87.513
186	6.659	227	31.619	268	71.316	309	87.750
187	6.970	228	32.189	269	72.516	310	87.991
188	7.327	229	32.793	270	73.627	311	88.267
189	7.734	230	33.400	271	74.636	312	88.562

Score	%ile	Score	%ile	Score	%ile	Score	%ile
313	88.847	353	93.044	393	95.621	433	98.817
314	89.123	354	93.098	394	95.718	434	98.831
315	89.437	355	93.154	395	95.835	435	98.839
316	89.741	356	93.207	396	95.945	436	98.846
317	90.002	357	93.266	397	96.026	437	98.848
318	90.284	358	93.314	398	96.123	438	98.856
319	90.553	359	93.365	399	96.206	439	98.861
320	90.808	360	93.431	400	96.293	440	98.866
321	91.000	361	93.485	401	96.366	441	98.872
322	91.202	362	93.535	402	96.426	442	98.874
323	91.380	363	93.596	403	96.507	443	98.880
324	91.517	364	93.658	404	96.588	444	98.882
325	91.647	365	93.720	405	96.691	445	98.887
326	91.754	366	93.786	406	96.777	446	98.890
327	91.848	367	93.845	407	96.866	447	98.895
328	91.936	368	93.898	408	96.935	448	98.898
329	91.992	369	93.971	409	97.035	449	98.901
330	92.044	370	94.020	410	97.128	450	98.906
331	92.091	371	94.076	411	97.230	451	98.912
332	92.128	372	94.129	412	97.335	452	98.917
333	92.167	373	94.190	413	97.439	453	98.920
334	92.200	374	94.246	414	97.573	454	98.921
335	92.229	375	94.297	415	97.676	455	98.926
336	92.257	376	94.351	416	97.790	456	98.927
337	92.290	377	94.397	417	97.890	457	98.929
338	92.325	378	94.444	418	97.991	458	98.933
339	92.361	379	94.513	419	98.086	459	98.938
340	92.396	380	94.559	420	98.173	460	98.944
341	92.428	381	94.600	421	98.249	461	98.946
342	92.469	382	94.660	422	98.332	462	98.952
343	92.506	383	94.712	423	98.422	463	98.956
344	92.548	384	94.776	424	98.487	464	98.960
345	92.588	385	94.835	425	98.551	465	98.967
346	92.640	386	94.926	426	98.599	466	98.971
347	92.697	387	95.019	427	98.656	467	98.977
348	92.749	388	95.101	428	98.699	468	98.982
349	92.810	389	95.188	429	98.737	469	98.990
350	92.862	390	95.302	430	98.771	470	98.999
351	92.924	391	95.409	431	98.793		
352	92.985	392	95.507	432	98.806	>470	>99.000

The YAHTZEE Score Distribution

This figure represents the results of a simulation of 100,000 games using the optimal strategy for YAHTZEE. Note that scores less than 100 or greater than 450 are very unlikely. The various peaks and valleys are due to the discrete scoring nature of the categories. For example, you will score either 25 or 0 for a full house, 35 or 0 for the Upper Section bonus, or 50 or 0 for a YAHTZEE. This figure provides a graphic depiction of how a given score compares to the universe of possible scores.

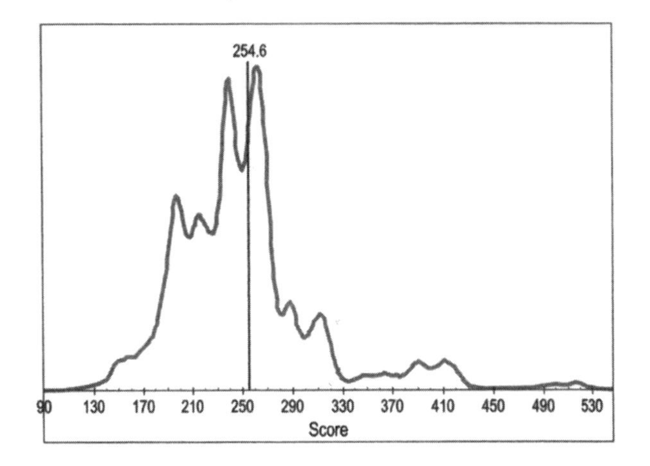

Appendix II
Sample Games With Annotations

The following samples are representations of actual games. The rolls were generated randomly and the games played by the computer according to the optimal strategy.

Sample Game #1

Hand #1

Here, there's not much else to save.

A simple decision here also.

Final Roll:

This is one of the game's classic toughies. Should the 5-5-5-5 be used as 4-of-a-kind or as Fives in the Upper Section. It's best to use them in the Upper Section and move comfortably ahead in the quest for the bonus.

UPPER SECTION	HOW TO SCORE	
Aces ⚀ = 1	Count and Add Only Aces	
Twos ⚁ = 2	Count and Add Only Twos	
Threes ⚂ = 3	Count and Add Only Threes	
Fours ⚃ = 4	Count and Add Only Fours	
Fives ⚄ = 5	Count and Add Only Fives	20
Sixes ⚅ = 6	Count and Add Only Sixes	
TOTAL SCORE	⟶	
BONUS	If total score is 63 or over SCORE 35	
TOTAL	Of Upper Section ⟶	

LOWER SECTION		
3-of-a-kind	Add Total of All Dice	
4-of-a-kind	Add Total of All Dice	
Full House	SCORE 25	
Sm. Straight	Sequence of 4 SCORE 30	
Lg. Straight	Sequence of 5 SCORE 40	
YAHTZEE	5-of-a-kind SCORE 50	
Chance	Score Total of All 5 Dice	
YAHTZEE BONUS	✔ FOR EACH BONUS	
	SCORE 100 PER ✔	
TOTAL	Of Lower Section ⟶	
TOTAL	Of Upper Section ⟶	
GRAND TOTAL	⟶	

Running score:	**20**
Upper Section: (relative to par)	**+5**

Hand #2

First Roll:

Hold:

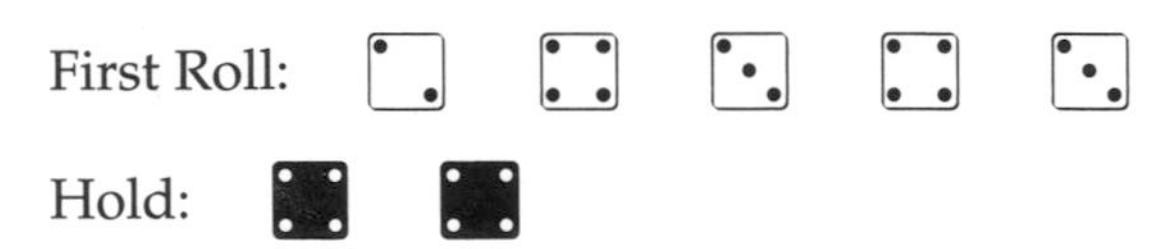

Early on, always keep the high pair when dealt two pairs with both corresponding Upper Section entries unfilled.

Second Roll:

Hold:

Things are looking good.

Final Roll:

Early in the game, it's best to use a 3-of-a-kind as an Upper Section entry.

UPPER SECTION	HOW TO SCORE	
Aces ⚀ = 1	Count and Add Only Aces	
Twos ⚁ = 2	Count and Add Only Twos	
Threes ⚂ = 3	Count and Add Only Threes	
Fours ⚃ = 4	Count and Add Only Fours	12
Fives ⚄ = 5	Count and Add Only Fives	20
Sixes ⚅ = 6	Count and Add Only Sixes	
TOTAL SCORE	→	
BONUS	If total score is 63 or over SCORE 35	
TOTAL	Of Upper Section →	

LOWER SECTION		
3-of-a-kind	Add Total of All Dice	
4-of-a-kind	Add Total of All Dice	
Full House	SCORE 25	
Sm. Straight	Sequence of 4 SCORE 30	
Lg. Straight	Sequence of 5 SCORE 40	
YAHTZEE	5-of-a-kind SCORE 50	
Chance	Score Total of All 5 Dice	
YAHTZEE BONUS	✔ FOR EACH BONUS	
	SCORE 100 PER ✔	
TOTAL	Of Lower Section →	
TOTAL	Of Upper Section →	
GRAND TOTAL	→	

Running score: **32**

Upper Section: **+5**
(relative to par)

Hand #3

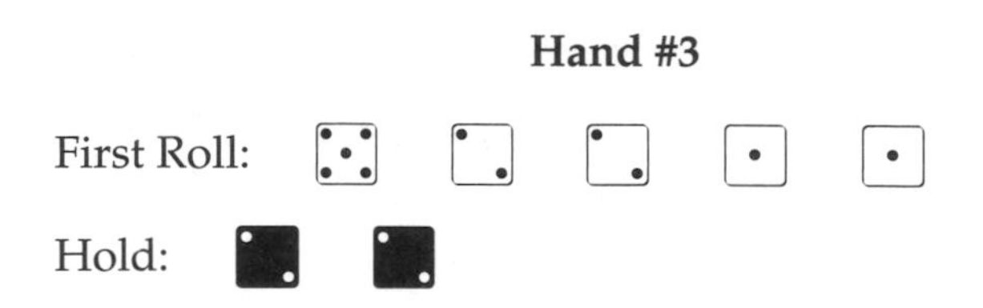

As before, always keep the high pair when dealt two pairs with both corresponding Upper Section entries unfilled.

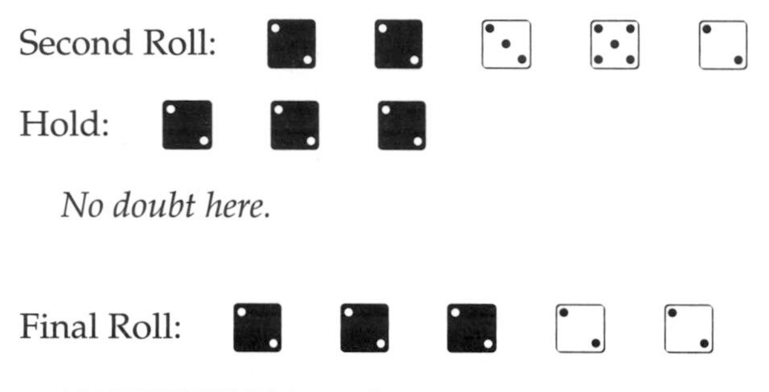

No doubt here.

YAHTZEE! This one's easy to score.

UPPER SECTION	HOW TO SCORE	
Aces ⚀ = 1	Count and Add Only Aces	
Twos ⚁ = 2	Count and Add Only Twos	
Threes ⚂ = 3	Count and Add Only Threes	
Fours ⚃ = 4	Count and Add Only Fours	12
Fives ⚄ = 5	Count and Add Only Fives	20
Sixes ⚅ = 6	Count and Add Only Sixes	
TOTAL SCORE	⟶	
BONUS	If total score is 63 or over SCORE 35	
TOTAL	Of Upper Section ⟶	

LOWER SECTION		
3-of-a-kind	Add Total of All Dice	
4-of-a-kind	Add Total of All Dice	
Full House	SCORE 25	
Sm. Straight	Sequence of 4 SCORE 30	
Lg. Straight	Sequence of 5 SCORE 40	
YAHTZEE	5-of-a-kind SCORE 50	50
Chance	Score Total of All 5 Dice	
YAHTZEE BONUS	✔ FOR EACH BONUS	
	SCORE 100 PER ✔	
TOTAL	Of Lower Section ⟶	
TOTAL	Of Upper Section ⟶	
GRAND TOTAL	⟶	

Running score:	**82**
Upper Section: (relative to par)	**+5**

Hand #4

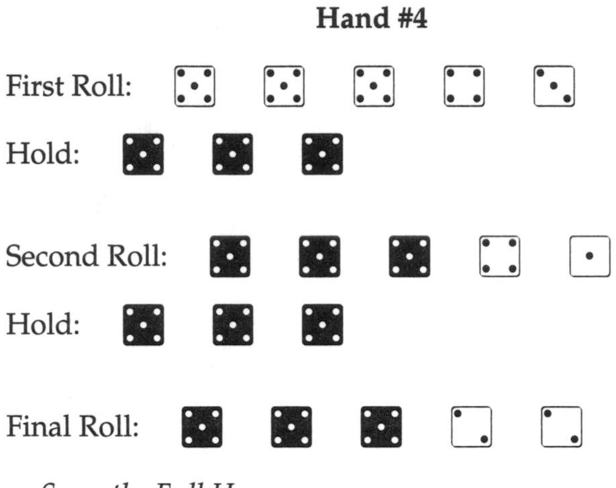

Score the Full House.

UPPER SECTION	HOW TO SCORE	
Aces ⚀ = 1	Count and Add Only Aces	
Twos ⚁ = 2	Count and Add Only Twos	
Threes ⚂ = 3	Count and Add Only Threes	
Fours ⚃ = 4	Count and Add Only Fours	**12**
Fives ⚄ = 5	Count and Add Only Fives	**20**
Sixes ⚅ = 6	Count and Add Only Sixes	
TOTAL SCORE	→	
BONUS	If total score is 63 or over SCORE 35	
TOTAL	Of Upper Section →	

LOWER SECTION		
3-of-a-kind	Add Total of All Dice	
4-of-a-kind	Add Total of All Dice	
Full House	SCORE 25	**25**
Sm. Straight	Sequence of 4 SCORE 30	
Lg. Straight	Sequence of 5 SCORE 40	
YAHTZEE	5-of-a-kind SCORE 50	**50**
Chance	Score Total of All 5 Dice	
YAHTZEE BONUS	✔ FOR EACH BONUS	
	SCORE 100 PER ✔	
TOTAL	Of Lower Section →	
TOTAL	Of Upper Section →	
GRAND TOTAL	→	

Running score:	**107**
Upper Section: (relative to par)	**+5**

Hand #5

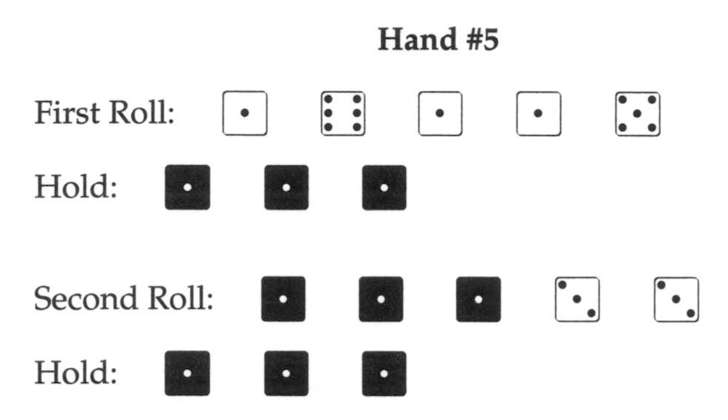

The Full House is already filled, so go for more aces.

Score three Aces in the Upper Section. As discussed in Chapter 6, 3-of-a-kind always goes in the Upper Section early. Plus, three 1s is a terrible combination to use as a Lower Section 3-of-a-kind.

UPPER SECTION	HOW TO SCORE	
Aces ⚀ = 1	Count and Add Only Aces	3
Twos ⚁ = 2	Count and Add Only Twos	
Threes ⚂ = 3	Count and Add Only Threes	
Fours ⚃ = 4	Count and Add Only Fours	12
Fives ⚄ = 5	Count and Add Only Fives	20
Sixes ⚅ = 6	Count and Add Only Sixes	
TOTAL SCORE	→	
BONUS	If total score is 63 or over SCORE 35	
TOTAL	Of Upper Section →	

LOWER SECTION			
3-of-a-kind	Add Total of All Dice		
4-of-a-kind	Add Total of All Dice		
Full House	SCORE 25	25	
Sm. Straight	Sequence of 4 SCORE 30		
Lg. Straight	Sequence of 5 SCORE 40		
YAHTZEE	5-of-a-kind SCORE 50	50	
Chance	Score Total of All 5 Dice		
YAHTZEE BONUS	✔ FOR EACH BONUS		
	SCORE 100 PER ✔		
TOTAL	Of Lower Section →		
TOTAL	Of Upper Section →		
GRAND TOTAL	→		

Running score:	**110**
Upper Section: (relative to par)	**+5**

Hand #6

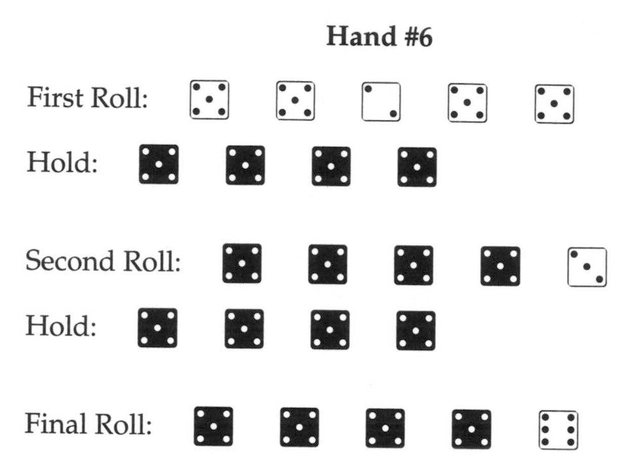

This hand is straightforward. Too bad a fifth 5 didn't show. The 26 points are applied to 4-of-a-kind.

UPPER SECTION	HOW TO SCORE	
Aces ⚀ = 1	Count and Add Only Aces	3
Twos ⚁ = 2	Count and Add Only Twos	
Threes ⚂ = 3	Count and Add Only Threes	
Fours ⚃ = 4	Count and Add Only Fours	12
Fives ⚄ = 5	Count and Add Only Fives	20
Sixes ⚅ = 6	Count and Add Only Sixes	
TOTAL SCORE	⟶	
BONUS	If total score is 63 or over SCORE 35	
TOTAL	Of Upper Section ⟶	

LOWER SECTION		
3-of-a-kind	Add Total of All Dice	
4-of-a-kind	Add Total of All Dice	26
Full House	SCORE 25	25
Sm. Straight	Sequence of 4 SCORE 30	
Lg. Straight	Sequence of 5 SCORE 40	
YAHTZEE	5-of-a-kind SCORE 50	50
Chance	Score Total of All 5 Dice	
YAHTZEE BONUS	✔ FOR EACH BONUS	
	SCORE 100 PER ✔	
TOTAL	Of Lower Section ⟶	
TOTAL	Of Upper Section ⟶	
GRAND TOTAL	⟶	

Running score:	**136**
Upper Section: **(relative to par)**	**+5**

Hand #7

First Roll:

Hold:

Don't hold the pair of 1s with the Aces box already filled. A hand of multiple 6s will be needed eventually, so now is as good a time as any to try for it.

Due to being comfortably ahead in the Upper Section, it's best to put these three 6s on top to solidify the position.

UPPER SECTION	HOW TO SCORE	
Aces ⚀ = 1	Count and Add Only Aces	3
Twos ⚁ = 2	Count and Add Only Twos	
Threes ⚂ = 3	Count and Add Only Threes	
Fours ⚃ = 4	Count and Add Only Fours	12
Fives ⚄ = 5	Count and Add Only Fives	20
Sixes ⚅ = 6	Count and Add Only Sixes	18
TOTAL SCORE	→	
BONUS	If total score is 63 or over SCORE 35	
TOTAL	Of Upper Section →	

LOWER SECTION		
3-of-a-kind	Add Total of All Dice	
4-of-a-kind	Add Total of All Dice	26
Full House	SCORE 25	25
Sm. Straight	Sequence of 4 SCORE 30	
Lg. Straight	Sequence of 5 SCORE 40	
YAHTZEE	5-of-a-kind SCORE 50	50
Chance	Score Total of All 5 Dice	
YAHTZEE BONUS	✔ FOR EACH BONUS	
	SCORE 100 PER ✔	
TOTAL	Of Lower Section →	
TOTAL	Of Upper Section →	
GRAND TOTAL	→	

Running score:	**154**
Upper Section: (relative to par)	**+5**

Hand #8

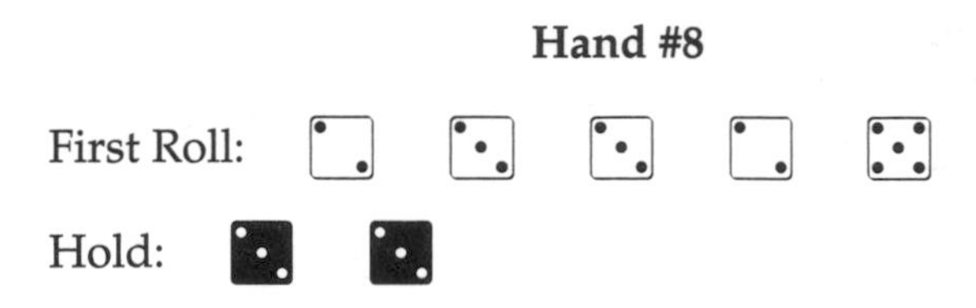

Hold the high pair when two pairs are rolled (and both Upper Section categories are unfilled).

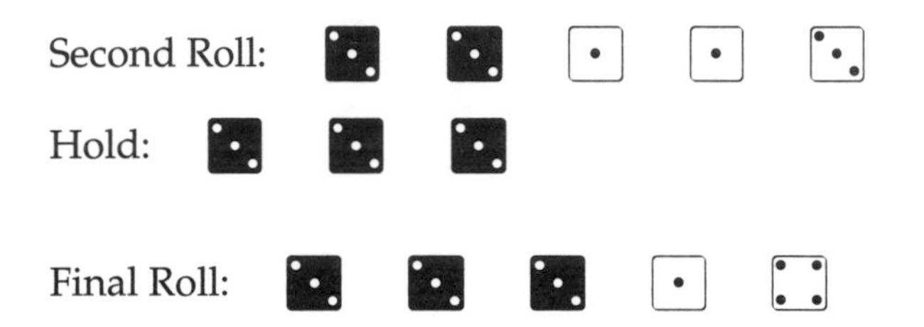

Final Roll:

The 3s go in the Upper Section for two reasons. First, it maintains the edge for the 35-point bonus. Second, the total of 14 is too low to be used for 3-of-a-kind. Generally, in the early to middle part of the game, the 3-of-a-kind entry should be filled with a total that contains three or more 5s and 6s, and only after the corresponding Upper Section box is filled.

UPPER SECTION	HOW TO SCORE	
Aces ⚀ = 1	Count and Add Only Aces	3
Twos ⚁ = 2	Count and Add Only Twos	
Threes ⚂ = 3	Count and Add Only Threes	9
Fours ⚃ = 4	Count and Add Only Fours	12
Fives ⚄ = 5	Count and Add Only Fives	20
Sixes ⚅ = 6	Count and Add Only Sixes	18
TOTAL SCORE	⟶	
BONUS	If total score is 63 or over SCORE 35	
TOTAL	Of Upper Section ⟶	

LOWER SECTION		
3-of-a-kind	Add Total of All Dice	
4-of-a-kind	Add Total of All Dice	26
Full House	SCORE 25	25
Sm. Straight	Sequence of 4 SCORE 30	
Lg. Straight	Sequence of 5 SCORE 40	
YAHTZEE	5-of-a-kind SCORE 50	50
Chance	Score Total of All 5 Dice	
YAHTZEE BONUS	✔ FOR EACH BONUS	
	SCORE 100 PER ✔	
TOTAL	Of Lower Section ⟶	
TOTAL	Of Upper Section ⟶	
GRAND TOTAL	⟶	

Running score:	**163**
Upper Section: (relative to par)	**+5**

Hand #9

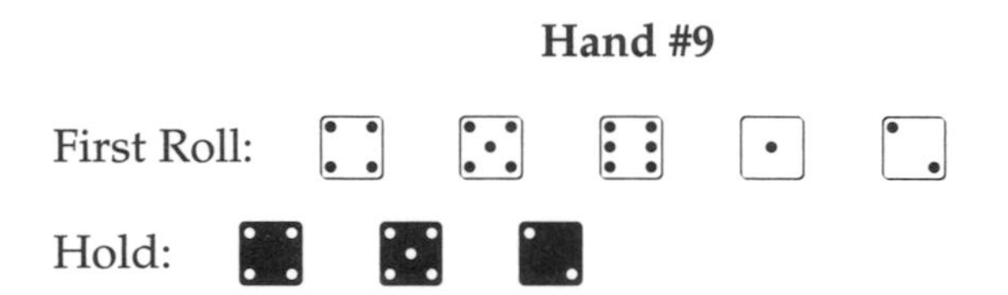

This is a very difficult hand to play correctly. However, it's easier to understand the correct play when you realize that the Upper Section bonus is already guaranteed (with a single 2). Hence, it's best to try for a Small or a Large Straight. Failing to get them at this point costs nothing.

You'll gladly take the Large Straight and forfeit the final roll.

UPPER SECTION	HOW TO SCORE	
Aces ⚀ = 1	Count and Add Only Aces	3
Twos ⚁ = 2	Count and Add Only Twos	
Threes ⚂ = 3	Count and Add Only Threes	9
Fours ⚃ = 4	Count and Add Only Fours	12
Fives ⚄ = 5	Count and Add Only Fives	20
Sixes ⚅ = 6	Count and Add Only Sixes	18
TOTAL SCORE	→	
BONUS	If total score is 63 or over SCORE 35	
TOTAL	Of Upper Section →	

LOWER SECTION		
3-of-a-kind	Add Total of All Dice	
4-of-a-kind	Add Total of All Dice	26
Full House	SCORE 25	25
Sm. Straight	Sequence of 4 SCORE 30	
Lg. Straight	Sequence of 5 SCORE 40	40
YAHTZEE	5-of-a-kind SCORE 50	50
Chance	Score Total of All 5 Dice	
YAHTZEE BONUS	✔ FOR EACH BONUS	
	SCORE 100 PER ✔	
TOTAL	Of Lower Section →	
TOTAL	Of Upper Section →	
GRAND TOTAL	→	

Running score: 203

Upper Section: (relative to par) +5

Hand #10

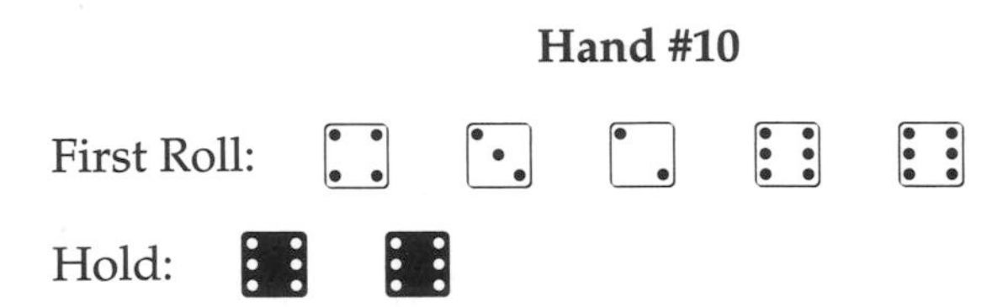

At this point in the game, it's time to start playing according to what's still open on the scorecard. The good news is Chance is still open, which accommodates fairly aggressive play. With the two 6s, the target is the 3-of-a-kind. There's no reason to worry about the Twos, since just one 2 will secure the Upper Section bonus (the table on page 59 shows that there's a 93.51% probability of making a single 2 even when waiting until the last hand). There's also no need to worry about the Small Straight, which occurs relatively frequently.

The four 6s are scored as 27 for an excellent 3-of-a-kind entry.

UPPER SECTION	HOW TO SCORE	
Aces ⚀ = 1	Count and Add Only Aces	3
Twos ⚁ = 2	Count and Add Only Twos	
Threes ⚂ = 3	Count and Add Only Threes	9
Fours ⚃ = 4	Count and Add Only Fours	12
Fives ⚄ = 5	Count and Add Only Fives	20
Sixes ⚅ = 6	Count and Add Only Sixes	18
TOTAL SCORE	→	
BONUS	If total score is 63 or over SCORE 35	
TOTAL	Of Upper Section →	

LOWER SECTION		
3-of-a-kind	Add Total of All Dice	27
4-of-a-kind	Add Total of All Dice	26
Full House	SCORE 25	25
Sm. Straight	Sequence of 4 SCORE 30	
Lg. Straight	Sequence of 5 SCORE 40	40
YAHTZEE	5-of-a-kind SCORE 50	50
Chance	Score Total of All 5 Dice	
YAHTZEE BONUS	✔ FOR EACH BONUS	
	SCORE 100 PER ✔	
TOTAL	Of Lower Section →	
TOTAL	Of Upper Section →	
GRAND TOTAL	→	

Running score: **230**

Upper Section: **+5**
(relative to par)

Hand #11

First Roll:

Hold:

This is another paradoxical play. It's best to keep the 2 to ensure the upper scorecard bonus (as discussed previously). The single 4 is kept to preserve a shot at the Small Straight.

The trip 2s are strong enough to change gears and take a shot at another YAHTZEE. The worst that can happen is the securing of the Upper Section bonus and a higher-than-expected score in the Twos.

Final Roll:

Complete the Upper Section with 8 points in the Twos; the Upper Section bonus is secured.

UPPER SECTION	HOW TO SCORE	
Aces ⚀ = 1	Count and Add Only Aces	3
Twos ⚁ = 2	Count and Add Only Twos	8
Threes ⚂ = 3	Count and Add Only Threes	9
Fours ⚃ = 4	Count and Add Only Fours	12
Fives ⚄ = 5	Count and Add Only Fives	20
Sixes ⚅ = 6	Count and Add Only Sixes	18
TOTAL SCORE	⟶	70
BONUS	If total score is 63 or over SCORE 35	35
TOTAL	Of Upper Section ⟶	105

LOWER SECTION		
3-of-a-kind	Add Total of All Dice	27
4-of-a-kind	Add Total of All Dice	26
Full House	SCORE 25	25
Sm. Straight	Sequence of 4 SCORE 30	
Lg. Straight	Sequence of 5 SCORE 40	40
YAHTZEE	5-of-a-kind SCORE 50	50
Chance	Score Total of All 5 Dice	
YAHTZEE BONUS	✔ FOR EACH BONUS	
	SCORE 100 PER ✔	
TOTAL	Of Lower Section ⟶	
TOTAL	Of Upper Section ⟶	
GRAND TOTAL	⟶	

Running score:	**238**
Upper Section: (relative to par)	**Bonus secured**

Hand #12

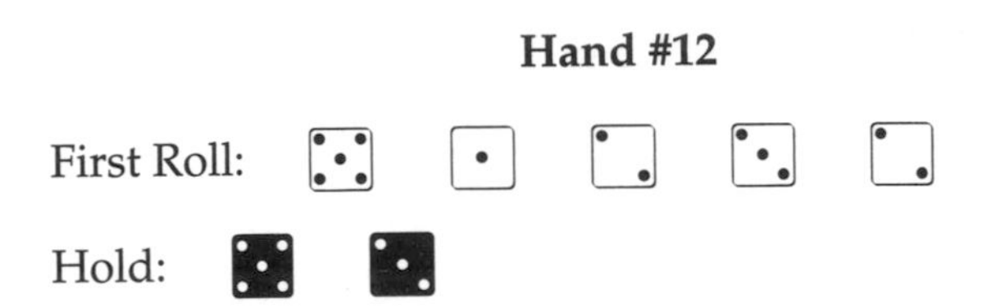

Yet another paradox. Keep in mind that at this late stage, play must be tailored based on the unfilled boxes. Hence, the Small Straight is the goal. The reason the 5-3 is kept (instead of, say, 1-2-3 or 2-3) is to maximize the value of Chance should the Small Straight not be made.

Record 30 for the 3-4-5-6 Small Straight. There's no reason to take the third roll since even a 6 would not dictate switching to Chance at this point.

UPPER SECTION		HOW TO SCORE	
Aces	⚀ = 1	Count and Add Only Aces	3
Twos	⚁ = 2	Count and Add Only Twos	8
Threes	⚂ = 3	Count and Add Only Threes	9
Fours	⚃ = 4	Count and Add Only Fours	12
Fives	⚄ = 5	Count and Add Only Fives	20
Sixes	⚅ = 6	Count and Add Only Sixes	18
TOTAL SCORE		→	70
BONUS		If total score is 63 or over SCORE 35	35
TOTAL		Of Upper Section →	105

LOWER SECTION		
3-of-a-kind	Add Total of All Dice	27
4-of-a-kind	Add Total of All Dice	26
Full House	SCORE 25	25
Sm. Straight	Sequence of 4 SCORE 30	30
Lg. Straight	Sequence of 5 SCORE 40	40
YAHTZEE	5-of-a-kind SCORE 50	50
Chance	Score Total of All 5 Dice	
YAHTZEE BONUS	✔ FOR EACH BONUS	
	SCORE 100 PER ✔	
TOTAL	Of Lower Section →	
TOTAL	Of Upper Section →	
GRAND TOTAL	→	

Running score:	**268**
Upper Section: (relative to par)	**Bonus secured**

Hand #13

First Roll:

Hold:

Normally, with only the Chance entry left unfilled, it's correct to keep all dice of 5 or more on the first roll and all dice of 4 or more on the second roll. The reason the 4s are held here is the power of the potential YAHTZEE and its 100-point bonus.

Second Roll:

Hold:

Final Roll:

Chance is filled with a score of 22.

UPPER SECTION		HOW TO SCORE	
Aces	⚀ = 1	Count and Add Only Aces	3
Twos	⚁ = 2	Count and Add Only Twos	8
Threes	⚂ = 3	Count and Add Only Threes	9
Fours	⚃ = 4	Count and Add Only Fours	12
Fives	⚄ = 5	Count and Add Only Fives	20
Sixes	⚅ = 6	Count and Add Only Sixes	18
TOTAL SCORE		→	70
BONUS		If total score is 63 or over SCORE 35	35
TOTAL		Of Upper Section →	105

LOWER SECTION			
3-of-a-kind		Add Total of All Dice	27
4-of-a-kind		Add Total of All Dice	26
Full House		SCORE 25	25
Sm. Straight	Sequence of 4	SCORE 30	30
Lg. Straight	Sequence of 5	SCORE 40	40
YAHTZEE	5-of-a-kind	SCORE 50	50
Chance		Score Total of All 5 Dice	22
YAHTZEE BONUS		✔ FOR EACH BONUS	
		SCORE 100 PER ✔	
TOTAL		Of Lower Section →	220
TOTAL		Of Upper Section →	105
GRAND TOTAL		→	325

The total score for this game is an impressive 325 points. The reasons for the above-average tally, which falls within the top 10% of scores are several: A YAHTZEE was achieved, the Upper Section bonus was secured, and no scoreboxes were filled with 0s.

Sample Game #2

Hand #1

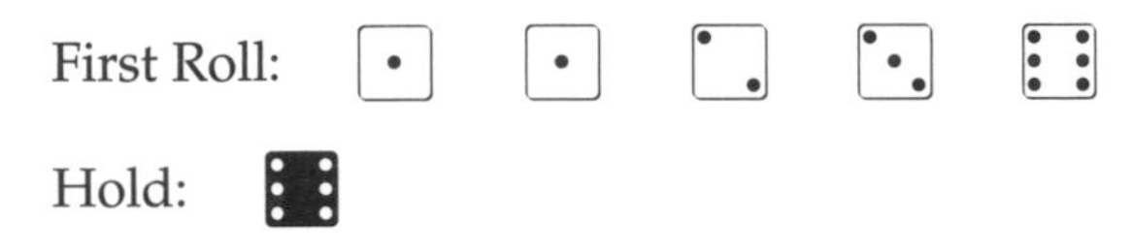

An important strategic move comes early, as a single 6 is held over a pair of 1s. The astute reader will note that there is nothing in the basic strategy that would lead to this move. But remember, the basic strategy, by definition, is not the optimal strategy, which is being applied in this game by a computer. In this case, there are two exceptions to keeping the pair of 1s, and they occur when there is either a 5 or a 6 kicker (in the same situation after the second roll, it's correct to keep the 1s).

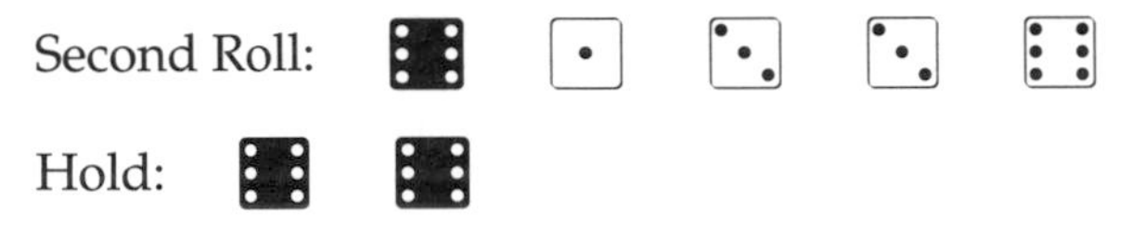

With two pair, we keep the high pair.

Final Roll:

A tough result right off the bat. Scoring the two Sixes will damage the quest for the Upper Section bonus considerably, so an alternative must be chosen. Refer back to the "Tough-Luck Hands" list on page 44, which indicates that the Chance total of 19 is inferior to recording the single Ace, which is the optimal way to score this hand.

UPPER SECTION	HOW TO SCORE	
Aces ⚀ = 1	Count and Add Only Aces	1
Twos ⚁ = 2	Count and Add Only Twos	
Threes ⚂ = 3	Count and Add Only Threes	
Fours ⚃ = 4	Count and Add Only Fours	
Fives ⚄ = 5	Count and Add Only Fives	
Sixes ⚅ = 6	Count and Add Only Sixes	
TOTAL SCORE	⟶	
BONUS	If total score is 63 or over SCORE 35	
TOTAL	Of Upper Section ⟶	

LOWER SECTION		
3-of-a-kind	Add Total of All Dice	
4-of-a-kind	Add Total of All Dice	
Full House	SCORE 25	
Sm. Straight	Sequence of 4 SCORE 30	
Lg. Straight	Sequence of 5 SCORE 40	
YAHTZEE	5-of-a-kind SCORE 50	
Chance	Score Total of All 5 Dice	
YAHTZEE BONUS	✔ FOR EACH BONUS	
	SCORE 100 PER ✔	
TOTAL	Of Lower Section ⟶	
TOTAL	Of Upper Section ⟶	
GRAND TOTAL	⟶	

Running score: 1

Upper Section: –2
(relative to par)

Hand #2

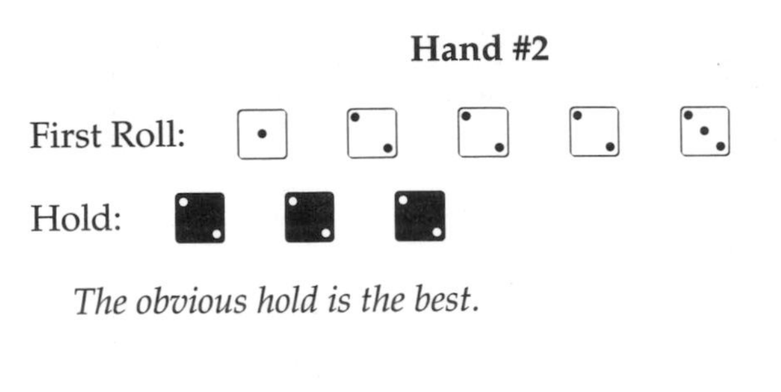

The obvious hold is the best.

Take the Full House. Note that if there had been three 4s, 5s, or three 6s, the correct play would be to keep the high trips and throw away the Full House.

UPPER SECTION	HOW TO SCORE	
Aces ⚀ = 1	Count and Add Only Aces	1
Twos ⚁ = 2	Count and Add Only Twos	
Threes ⚂ = 3	Count and Add Only Threes	
Fours ⚃ = 4	Count and Add Only Fours	
Fives ⚄ = 5	Count and Add Only Fives	
Sixes ⚅ = 6	Count and Add Only Sixes	
TOTAL SCORE	→	
BONUS	If total score is 63 or over SCORE 35	
TOTAL	Of Upper Section →	

LOWER SECTION		
3-of-a-kind	Add Total of All Dice	
4-of-a-kind	Add Total of All Dice	
Full House	SCORE 25	25
Sm. Straight	Sequence of 4 SCORE 30	
Lg. Straight	Sequence of 5 SCORE 40	
YAHTZEE	5-of-a-kind SCORE 50	
Chance	Score Total of All 5 Dice	
YAHTZEE BONUS	✔ FOR EACH BONUS	
	SCORE 100 PER ✔	
TOTAL	Of Lower Section →	
TOTAL	Of Upper Section →	
GRAND TOTAL	→	

Running score:	**26**
Upper Section: (relative to par)	**–2**

Hand #3

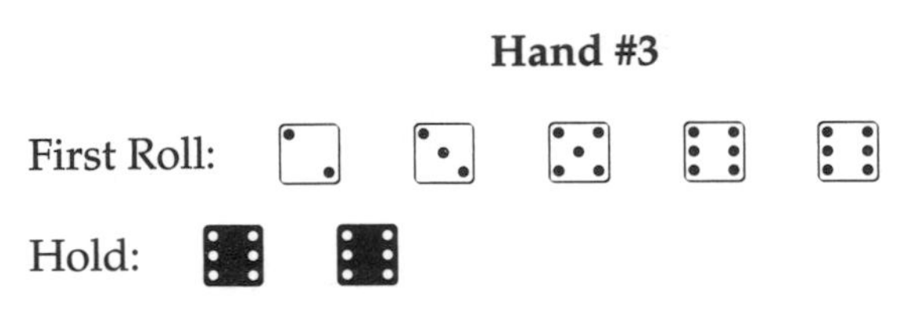

Follow the general rule of keeping the (high) pair.

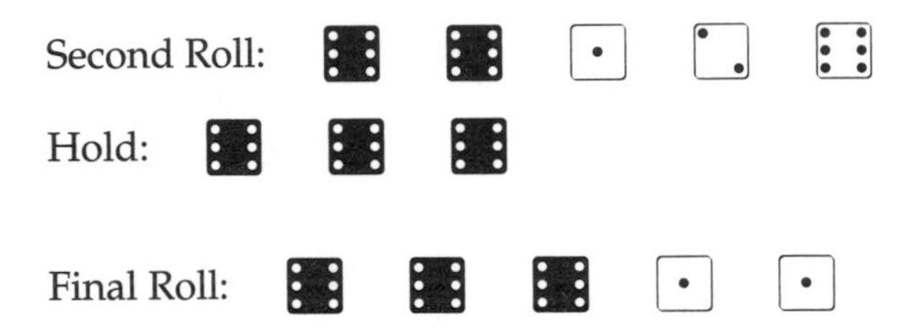

The Full House is already filled, so the major decision is whether to score this as Sixes or 3-of-a-kind. Early, it's best to score this hand in the Upper Section.

UPPER SECTION	HOW TO SCORE	
Aces ⚀ = 1	Count and Add Only Aces	1
Twos ⚁ = 2	Count and Add Only Twos	
Threes ⚂ = 3	Count and Add Only Threes	
Fours ⚃ = 4	Count and Add Only Fours	
Fives ⚄ = 5	Count and Add Only Fives	
Sixes ⚅ = 6	Count and Add Only Sixes	18
TOTAL SCORE	→	
BONUS	If total score is 63 or over SCORE 35	
TOTAL	Of Upper Section →	

LOWER SECTION		
3-of-a-kind	Add Total of All Dice	
4-of-a-kind	Add Total of All Dice	
Full House	SCORE 25	25
Sm. Straight	Sequence of 4 SCORE 30	
Lg. Straight	Sequence of 5 SCORE 40	
YAHTZEE	5-of-a-kind SCORE 50	
Chance	Score Total of All 5 Dice	
YAHTZEE BONUS	✔ FOR EACH BONUS	
	SCORE 100 PER ✔	
TOTAL	Of Lower Section →	
TOTAL	Of Upper Section →	
GRAND TOTAL	→	

Running score:	**44**
Upper Section: (relative to par)	**–2**

Hand #4

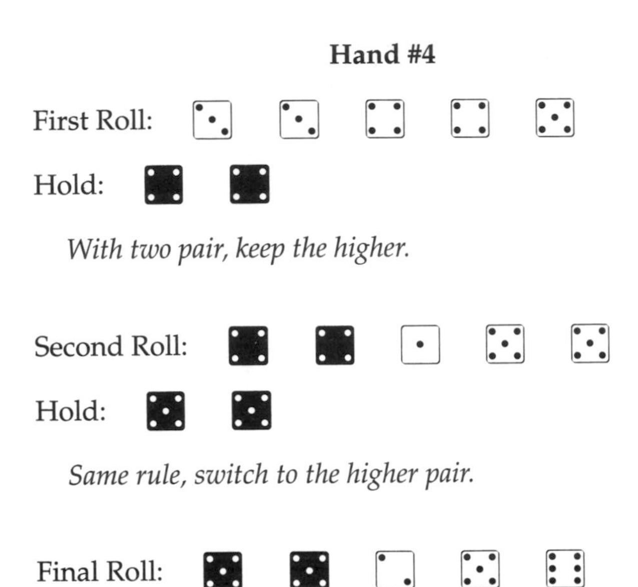

First Roll:

Hold:

With two pair, keep the higher.

Second Roll:

Hold:

Same rule, switch to the higher pair.

Final Roll:

The Fives are scored in the Upper Section.

UPPER SECTION		HOW TO SCORE	
Aces	⚀ = 1	Count and Add Only Aces	1
Twos	⚁ = 2	Count and Add Only Twos	
Threes	⚂ = 3	Count and Add Only Threes	
Fours	⚃ = 4	Count and Add Only Fours	
Fives	⚄ = 5	Count and Add Only Fives	15
Sixes	⚅ = 6	Count and Add Only Sixes	18
TOTAL SCORE		→	
BONUS		If total score is 63 or over SCORE 35	
TOTAL		Of Upper Section →	

LOWER SECTION			
3-of-a-kind		Add Total of All Dice	
4-of-a-kind		Add Total of All Dice	
Full House		SCORE 25	25
Sm. Straight	Sequence of 4	SCORE 30	
Lg. Straight	Sequence of 5	SCORE 40	
YAHTZEE	5-of-a-kind	SCORE 50	
Chance		Score Total of All 5 Dice	
YAHTZEE BONUS		✔ FOR EACH BONUS	
		SCORE 100 PER ✔	
TOTAL		Of Lower Section →	
TOTAL		Of Upper Section →	
GRAND TOTAL		→	

Running score:	**59**
Upper Section: (relative to par)	**–2**

Hand #5

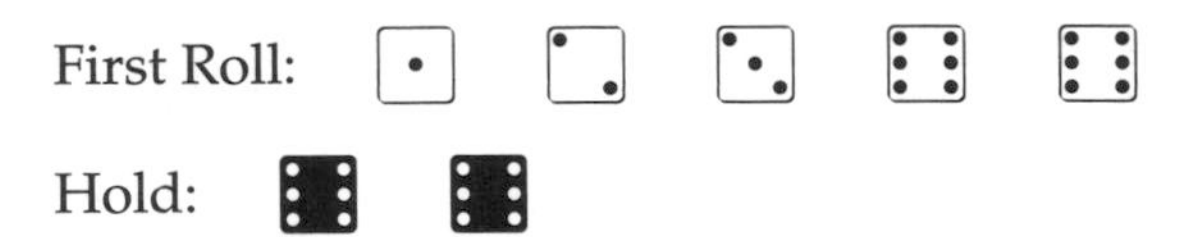

Again, keep the high pair. The goal here is to get a good 3-of-a-kind or better. The backup is Chance.

A surprise of sorts. The kicker 5 is kept because both 3-of-a-kind and Chance take into account the sum of all five dice. The risk from keeping the Five (slightly lowering the probability of obtaining 3-of-a-kind) is outweighed by its benefit in scoring.

Final Roll:

Didn't get it, but the total of 24 is quite good for Chance.

UPPER SECTION	HOW TO SCORE	
Aces ⚀ = 1	Count and Add Only Aces	1
Twos ⚁ = 2	Count and Add Only Twos	
Threes ⚂ = 3	Count and Add Only Threes	
Fours ⚃ = 4	Count and Add Only Fours	
Fives ⚄ = 5	Count and Add Only Fives	15
Sixes ⚅ = 6	Count and Add Only Sixes	18
TOTAL SCORE	⟶	
BONUS	If total score is 63 or over SCORE 35	
TOTAL	Of Upper Section ⟶	

LOWER SECTION		
3-of-a-kind	Add Total of All Dice	
4-of-a-kind	Add Total of All Dice	
Full House	SCORE 25	25
Sm. Straight	Sequence of 4 SCORE 30	
Lg. Straight	Sequence of 5 SCORE 40	
YAHTZEE	5-of-a-kind SCORE 50	
Chance	Score Total of All 5 Dice	24
YAHTZEE BONUS	✔ FOR EACH BONUS	
	SCORE 100 PER ✔	
TOTAL	Of Lower Section ⟶	
TOTAL	Of Upper Section ⟶	
GRAND TOTAL	⟶	

Running score:	**83**
Upper Section: (relative to par)	**–2**

Hand #6

Egad! A horrible first roll. There are no pairs, and the Fives and Sixes scoreboxes are filled. The best option is to try for a Straight. The 2-3-5 is preferred over the 2-3-5-6 because of the enhanced possibilities for a Small Straight.

A fortuitous roll yields the best possible result, the Large Straight.

UPPER SECTION	HOW TO SCORE	
Aces ⚀ = 1	Count and Add Only Aces	1
Twos ⚁ = 2	Count and Add Only Twos	
Threes ⚂ = 3	Count and Add Only Threes	
Fours ⚃ = 4	Count and Add Only Fours	
Fives ⚄ = 5	Count and Add Only Fives	15
Sixes ⚅ = 6	Count and Add Only Sixes	18
TOTAL SCORE	→	
BONUS	If total score is 63 or over SCORE 35	
TOTAL	Of Upper Section →	

LOWER SECTION		
3-of-a-kind	Add Total of All Dice	
4-of-a-kind	Add Total of All Dice	
Full House	SCORE 25	25
Sm. Straight	Sequence of 4 SCORE 30	
Lg. Straight	Sequence of 5 SCORE 40	40
YAHTZEE	5-of-a-kind SCORE 50	
Chance	Score Total of All 5 Dice	24
YAHTZEE BONUS	✔ FOR EACH BONUS	
	SCORE 100 PER ✔	
TOTAL	Of Lower Section →	
TOTAL	Of Upper Section →	
GRAND TOTAL	→	

Running score: **123**

Upper Section: **–2**
(relative to par)

Hand #7

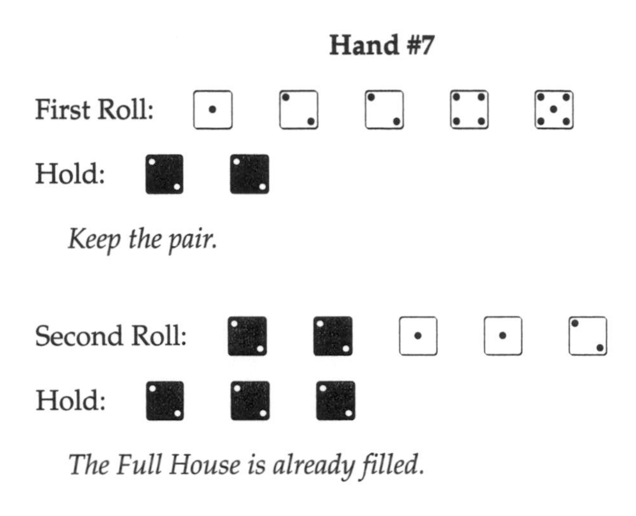

First Roll:

Hold:

Keep the pair.

Second Roll:

Hold:

The Full House is already filled.

Final Roll:

Even though the game is well into the middle stages and there's still a deficit in the Upper Section, there's no reason to panic. The Threes and Fours categories remain open, and one tally above par in either scorebox will make up the shortfall.

UPPER SECTION	HOW TO SCORE	
Aces ⚀ = 1	Count and Add Only Aces	1
Twos ⚁ = 2	Count and Add Only Twos	6
Threes ⚂ = 3	Count and Add Only Threes	
Fours ⚃ = 4	Count and Add Only Fours	
Fives ⚄ = 5	Count and Add Only Fives	15
Sixes ⚅ = 6	Count and Add Only Sixes	18
TOTAL SCORE	⟶	
BONUS	If total score is 63 or over SCORE 35	
TOTAL	Of Upper Section ⟶	

LOWER SECTION		
3-of-a-kind	Add Total of All Dice	
4-of-a-kind	Add Total of All Dice	
Full House	SCORE 25	25
Sm. Straight	Sequence of 4 SCORE 30	
Lg. Straight	Sequence of 5 SCORE 40	40
YAHTZEE	5-of-a-kind SCORE 50	
Chance	Score Total of All 5 Dice	24
YAHTZEE BONUS	✔ FOR EACH BONUS	
	SCORE 100 PER ✔	
TOTAL	Of Lower Section ⟶	
TOTAL	Of Upper Section ⟶	
GRAND TOTAL	⟶	

Running score:	**129**
Upper Section: (relative to par)	**–2**

Hand #8

First Roll:

Hold:

The Full House is filled, so it's best to try for 4-of-a-kind or YAHTZEE.

Score the 24 in 3-of-a-kind.

UPPER SECTION	HOW TO SCORE	
Aces ⚀ = 1	Count and Add Only Aces	1
Twos ⚁ = 2	Count and Add Only Twos	6
Threes ⚂ = 3	Count and Add Only Threes	
Fours ⚃ = 4	Count and Add Only Fours	
Fives ⚄ = 5	Count and Add Only Fives	15
Sixes ⚅ = 6	Count and Add Only Sixes	18
TOTAL SCORE	→	
BONUS	If total score is 63 or over SCORE 35	
TOTAL	Of Upper Section →	

LOWER SECTION		
3-of-a-kind	Add Total of All Dice	24
4-of-a-kind	Add Total of All Dice	
Full House	SCORE 25	25
Sm. Straight	Sequence of 4 SCORE 30	
Lg. Straight	Sequence of 5 SCORE 40	40
YAHTZEE	5-of-a-kind SCORE 50	
Chance	Score Total of All 5 Dice	24
YAHTZEE BONUS	✔ FOR EACH BONUS	
	SCORE 100 PER ✔	
TOTAL	Of Lower Section →	
TOTAL	Of Upper Section →	
GRAND TOTAL	→	

Running score: 153

Upper Section: –2
(relative to par)

Hand #9

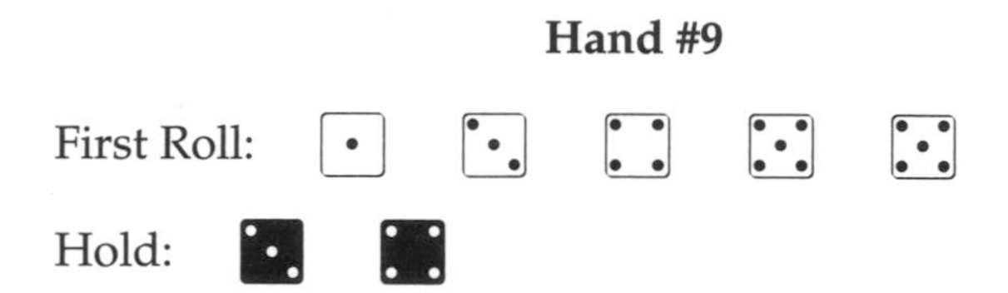

The Fives entry is filled (and it's unwise to try for four 5s when starting with only two), plus 3-of-a-kind and Chance are also filled. Hence, hold the 3-4 and go for the needed Upper Section categories of Threes and Fours or a Small Straight.

With the pair of 3s, the strategy is to try to fill the Threes scorebox.

Scoring 6 in the Threes scorebox might seem like the obvious strategy, but doing so would make it almost impossible to get the Upper Section bonus. With just four hands left to play, a YAHTZEE is unlikely, so the best play is to fill the YAHTZEE entry with 0 and preserve the potential Upper Section bonus.

UPPER SECTION	HOW TO SCORE	
Aces ⚀ = 1	Count and Add Only Aces	1
Twos ⚁ = 2	Count and Add Only Twos	6
Threes ⚂ = 3	Count and Add Only Threes	
Fours ⚃ = 4	Count and Add Only Fours	
Fives ⚄ = 5	Count and Add Only Fives	15
Sixes ⚅ = 6	Count and Add Only Sixes	18
TOTAL SCORE	→	
BONUS	If total score is 63 or over SCORE 35	
TOTAL	Of Upper Section →	

LOWER SECTION		
3-of-a-kind	Add Total of All Dice	24
4-of-a-kind	Add Total of All Dice	
Full House	SCORE 25	25
Sm. Straight	Sequence of 4 SCORE 30	
Lg. Straight	Sequence of 5 SCORE 40	40
YAHTZEE	5-of-a-kind SCORE 50	0
Chance	Score Total of All 5 Dice	24
YAHTZEE BONUS	✔ FOR EACH BONUS	
	SCORE 100 PER ✔	
TOTAL	Of Lower Section →	
TOTAL	Of Upper Section →	
GRAND TOTAL	→	

Running score:	**153**
Upper Section: (relative to par)	**–2**

Hand #10

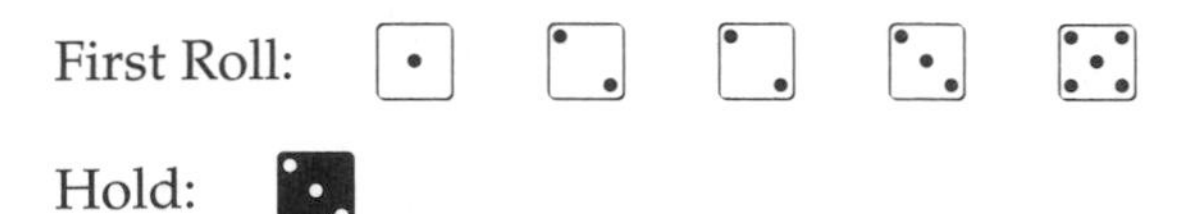

First Roll:

Hold:

Nearing the end of the game, it's time to start playing according to what's open on the scorecard. The deficit in the Upper Section is only 2 points. Hence, hold the solitary 3 in an effort to get four 3s.

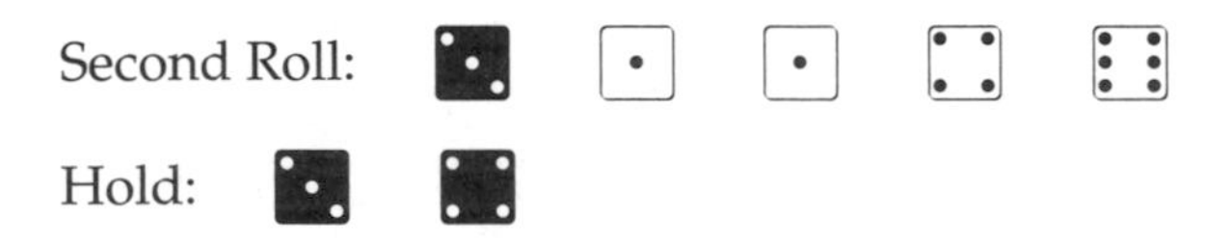

Second Roll:

Hold:

This maximizes the chances for a Small Straight while holding out hope for three or more 3s or 4s.

Final Roll:

Nothing helpful. It's now time to acknowledge that the Upper Section bonus is probably lost and fill the Fours.

UPPER SECTION	HOW TO SCORE	
Aces ⚀ = 1	Count and Add Only Aces	1
Twos ⚁ = 2	Count and Add Only Twos	6
Threes ⚂ = 3	Count and Add Only Threes	
Fours ⚃ = 4	Count and Add Only Fours	8
Fives ⚄ = 5	Count and Add Only Fives	15
Sixes ⚅ = 6	Count and Add Only Sixes	18
TOTAL SCORE	⟶	
BONUS	If total score is 63 or over SCORE 35	
TOTAL	Of Upper Section ⟶	

LOWER SECTION		
3-of-a-kind	Add Total of All Dice	24
4-of-a-kind	Add Total of All Dice	
Full House	SCORE 25	25
Sm. Straight	Sequence of 4 SCORE 30	
Lg. Straight	Sequence of 5 SCORE 40	40
YAHTZEE	5-of-a-kind SCORE 50	0
Chance	Score Total of All 5 Dice	24
YAHTZEE BONUS	✔ FOR EACH BONUS	
	SCORE 100 PER ✔	
TOTAL	Of Lower Section ⟶	
TOTAL	Of Upper Section ⟶	
GRAND TOTAL	⟶	

Running score:	**161**
Upper Section: (relative to par)	**–6**

Hand #11

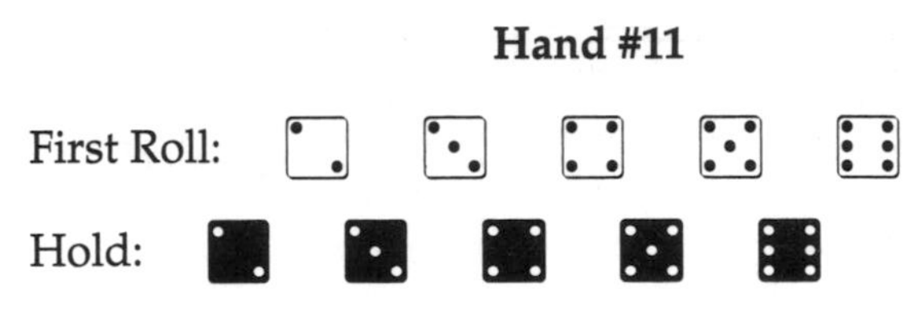

A gimme; score the Small Straight.

UPPER SECTION	HOW TO SCORE	
Aces ⚀ = 1	Count and Add Only Aces	**1**
Twos ⚁ = 2	Count and Add Only Twos	**6**
Threes ⚂ = 3	Count and Add Only Threes	
Fours ⚃ = 4	Count and Add Only Fours	**8**
Fives ⚄ = 5	Count and Add Only Fives	**15**
Sixes ⚅ = 6	Count and Add Only Sixes	**18**
TOTAL SCORE	⟶	
BONUS	If total score is 63 or over SCORE 35	
TOTAL	Of Upper Section ⟶	

LOWER SECTION		
3-of-a-kind	Add Total of All Dice	**24**
4-of-a-kind	Add Total of All Dice	
Full House	SCORE 25	**25**
Sm. Straight	Sequence of 4 SCORE 30	**30**
Lg. Straight	Sequence of 5 SCORE 40	**40**
YAHTZEE	5-of-a-kind SCORE 50	**0**
Chance	Score Total of All 5 Dice	**24**
YAHTZEE BONUS	✔ FOR EACH BONUS	
	SCORE 100 PER ✔	
TOTAL	Of Lower Section ⟶	
TOTAL	Of Upper Section ⟶	
GRAND TOTAL	⟶	

Running score:	**191**
Upper Section: (relative to par)	**–6**

Hand #12

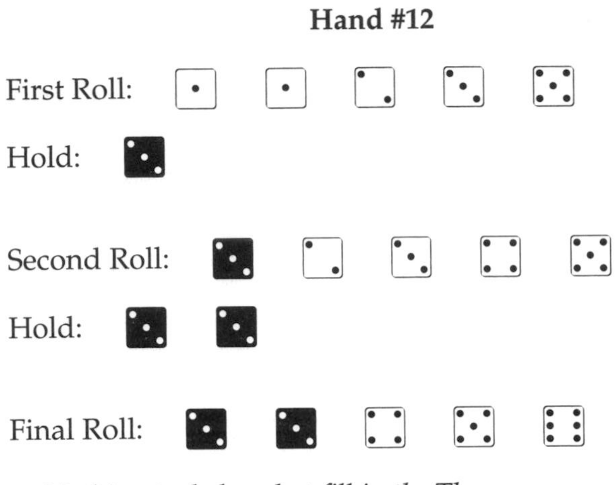

Nothing to do here but fill in the Threes.

UPPER SECTION		HOW TO SCORE	
Aces	⚀ = 1	Count and Add Only Aces	1
Twos	⚁ = 2	Count and Add Only Twos	6
Threes	⚂ = 3	Count and Add Only Threes	6
Fours	⚃ = 4	Count and Add Only Fours	8
Fives	⚄ = 5	Count and Add Only Fives	15
Sixes	⚅ = 6	Count and Add Only Sixes	18
TOTAL SCORE		→	54
BONUS		If total score is 63 or over SCORE 35	0
TOTAL		Of Upper Section →	54

LOWER SECTION			
3-of-a-kind		Add Total of All Dice	24
4-of-a-kind		Add Total of All Dice	
Full House		SCORE 25	25
Sm. Straight	Sequence of 4	SCORE 30	30
Lg. Straight	Sequence of 5	SCORE 40	40
YAHTZEE	5-of-a-kind	SCORE 50	0
Chance		Score Total of All 5 Dice	24
YAHTZEE BONUS		✔ FOR EACH BONUS	
		SCORE 100 PER ✔	
TOTAL		Of Lower Section →	
TOTAL		Of Upper Section →	
GRAND TOTAL		→	

Running score:	**197**
Upper Section: (relative to par)	**Bonus forfeited**

Hand #13

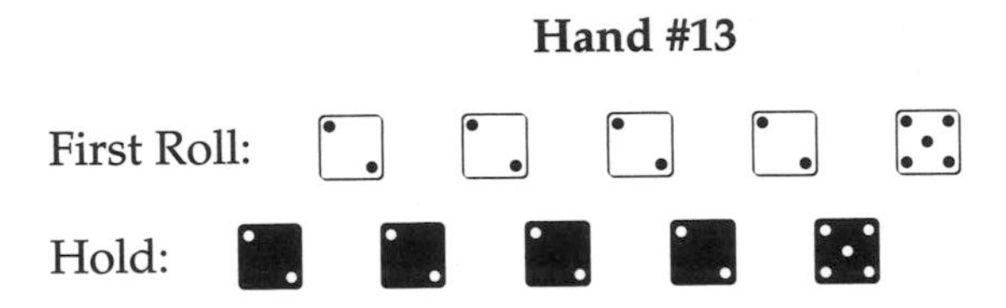

The only open category is 4-of-a-kind, so keep the four 2s. A YAHTZEE is worthless (it's already filled with 0), so the only possible improvement is a 6 kicker. Better to keep the 5 and score 13 for the hand.

UPPER SECTION		HOW TO SCORE	
Aces	⚀ = 1	Count and Add Only Aces	1
Twos	⚁ = 2	Count and Add Only Twos	6
Threes	⚂ = 3	Count and Add Only Threes	6
Fours	⚃ = 4	Count and Add Only Fours	8
Fives	⚄ = 5	Count and Add Only Fives	15
Sixes	⚅ = 6	Count and Add Only Sixes	18
TOTAL SCORE		⟶	54
BONUS		If total score is 63 or over SCORE 35	0
TOTAL		Of Upper Section ⟶	54

LOWER SECTION		
3-of-a-kind	Add Total of All Dice	24
4-of-a-kind	Add Total of All Dice	13
Full House	SCORE 25	25
Sm. Straight	Sequence of 4 SCORE 30	30
Lg. Straight	Sequence of 5 SCORE 40	40
YAHTZEE	5-of-a-kind SCORE 50	0
Chance	Score Total of All 5 Dice	24
YAHTZEE BONUS	✔ FOR EACH BONUS	
	SCORE 100 PER ✔	
TOTAL	Of Lower Section ⟶	156
TOTAL	Of Upper Section ⟶	54
GRAND TOTAL	⟶	210

A subaverage game total (falling at about the 21st percentile), but an informative game nonetheless. The main reason for the low score is the failure to earn the 35-point bonus. In reviewing the game, note the flexibility maintained in trying to salvage the Upper Section bonus until late in the game, when the quest was finally abandoned.

Appendix III
The YAHTZEE Solution

As divulged in Chapter 4, the key to solving YAHTZEE was to consider the game backward. This Appendix contains a more in-depth explanation of the procedure.

Starting with a completed scorecard (ignoring for the moment how the card has been completed, just as long as all the scoreboxes have been filled), we take a step backward and unfill one of the scoreboxes. We then ask ourselves how much that single entry is "worth" when left unfilled (its expected value assuming perfect play) and how we optimize the play of that last hand. To do this, again, we play the hand backward.

The hand is considered in three steps from end to beginning.

Step #1 — End of Hand
We begin by considering each of the 252 possible combinations of five dice as if it had occurred after the third and final roll with one unfilled entry. It's then straightforward to plug in the appropriate scorecard value (since only one category is unfilled). So, what we obtain is a value for each of the 252 possible combinations after the final roll. This value is saved.

Step #2 — After the Second Roll
We then take another step backward and separately consider each of the 252 possible combinations, determining how best to play each combination in the case that it represents our hand after the second roll. This requires considering all of the possible strategies for each combination.

For example, let's assume we're faced with 1-2-3-5-6 after the second roll. We must consider each of the possible strategies available to us, which are made up of the one way of holding all five dice, the five ways of holding four dice, the ten ways of holding three dice, and so forth (see Chapter 3).

For each combination, we sift through the possibilities and ascertain the value associated with implementing each strategy. This is done by calculating and considering the theoretical distribution of possible final rolls for each strategy, which, in turn, requires simply looking up the previously saved value from step #1. Thus, in Step #2, for each of the 252 combinations, we optimize by choosing the strategy that yields the greatest expected value. This value is saved.

Step #3 — After the First Roll

We then take a final step backward and consider each of the 252 combinations that may occur after the first roll. Proceeding here exactly as in Step #2, we consider all possible strategies, and choose the one with the greatest expected value. By properly weighting each of the initial combinations, we obtain the overall expected value for the hand.

To this point, we've solved how to play optimally with a single unfilled category (no matter which one). We may repeat this exercise with the rest of the categories, one at a time, to ascertain what each is worth when left as the sole unfilled scorebox.

We now step backward in time to consider two unfilled categories. This time we make use of our knowledge of how much each single unfilled category is worth to determine how to play with two unfilled. That is, with two unfilled categories, we can determine how to proceed by virtue of our previous work.

A playful analogy may be in order. Ask a physicist and a mathematician to move a plate from a table to a cupboard and they will each do so. Thereafter, if you ask each to move a plate from a dishwasher to a cupboard, the physicist will do so, but the mathematician will first move it to the table, because the subsequent move from the table to the cupboard is a problem that has already been solved.

Similarly, in this solution of YAHTZEE, we are continually making use of previous work to facilitate additional analysis. This technique of bootstrapping (using a previously determined answer to facilitate future computations) is used and reused as we continue to work our way backward in time. When we finally reach 13 unfilled categories (i.e., the beginning of the game), our work is done!

As discussed in Chapter 4, this technique of working backward saves an incredible number of computations that would otherwise need to be performed.

Another key attribute of YAHTZEE that facilitates the solution is the redundant nature of some of the scorecard categories. To illustrate, consider a situation in which the Aces has been scored as 2 and the Twos is scored as 6. This is mathematically equivalent to a situation in which both the Aces and the Twos are scored as 4. In each case, the Aces and Twos have been filled, and in each case the total of the two scoreboxes is 8 points. As such, they are mathematically equivalent, and the resultant optimal strategy is identical in both cases.

As another example, consider a game in which the Full House scorebox has been filled with 0, as opposed to a different game in which the Full House has been filled with 25. All else being equal, it turns out that the optimal strategy for each case is identical. Sure, it's always preferable to have made the Full House. But whether we have or not, as long as the scorebox is filled (whether with 0 or

25), the optimal way to play the remainder of the game is identical.

In terms of game paths, the redundancy is represented as branches that come to a common node, leading to a game position that (from that point forward in time) has the same optimal strategy, but (looking backward in time) may have been arrived at in many different ways.

In fact, the calculation is surprisingly tricky. We cannot truly go backward in time when playing the game. While the above description of optimal strategy with respect to a Full House is correct (it doesn't matter how Full House has been filled, only whether it has been filled or not), the same cannot be said for a YAHTZEE. Of course, it matters whether YAHTZEE has been filled or not, but it also matters how it has been filled. Specifically, there's a big difference whether this category has been filled with 50 or 0. In fact, optimal play will vary greatly depending on it. As you might imagine, if we've already made one YAHTZEE, we'll play more aggressively to try to get another and its attendant 100-point bonus. On the other hand, if we've already filled the scorebox with 0, there is almost no incentive for us to go for a YAHTZEE later in the game.

Remember also the 35-point bonus for the Upper Section. Playing a particular hand properly depends not only on which categories remain unfilled, but also on how close we are to 63 points in the Upper Section. In other words, we cannot, in principle, properly analyze the expected value for any hand unless we know the history of the game. But we can't know the game's history because we're traveling backward in time. What a conundrum!

The way out of this snafu is to consider all possible positions that could occur later in time. Thus, for a given set of unfilled categories, we continually consider the optimal way to play, assuming a) we've filled the YAHTZEE box with 50, b) we've filled the YAHTZEE box with 0, and

c) we've not yet filled the YAHTZEE box. (A similar approach is adopted for the 35-point bonus for the Upper Section.)

Considerations such as these just described lead to the second key to the solution, which is that only a "small" number of possible intermediate positions need to be considered in order to comprehend and analyze the complete scope of the game. This small number is about three-quarters of a million, estimated as the product 2^{12} (for the current state of which scorecard boxes are filled/unfilled excluding the YAHTZEE box) × 64 (for the current total in the Upper Section ranging from 0 to 63+) × 3 (for an indicator of the status of the YAHTZEE box filled with 50, filled with 0, or unfilled).

About the Author

OLAF VANCURA received his Ph.D. in physics from Johns Hopkins University in 1992. Subsequently, he joined the Harvard-Smithsonian Center for Astrophysics, and for several years taught the popular Casino Gambling curriculum at Tufts University. An inventor with over 60 U.S. patents, he currently designs and develops casino games for Game Ingenuity. Vancura is the coauthor, with Ken Fuchs, of *Knock-Out Blackjack: The Easiest Card-Counting System Ever Devised*.